A PARENTS'
GUIDE TO CHILD
DISCIPLINE

A PARENTS' GUIDE TO CHILD DISCIPLINE

By Rudolf Dreikurs, M.D., and
Loren Grey, Ph.D.

Hawthorn/Dutton New York

Library of Congress Catalog Card Number: 74-102418

ISBN: 0-8015-5736-4

Portions of *A Parents' Guide to Child Discipline*
originally appeared in
Logical Consequences: A New Approach to Discipline

14 15

CONTENTS

A PARENTS' GUIDE TO CHILD DISCIPLINE

CHAPTER 1

WHY IS A NEW TRADITION
IN CHILD REARING NEEDED?

In Southampton, Long Island, a group of 127 socialites gathered in a mansion for one of the season's most elaborate debutante parties. During the night they went on a rampage, ripping down chandeliers, breaking windows, and destroying furniture. Their explanation: they had none.

In East Los Angeles a carload of young hoodlums attacked a high school teacher and several students when asked to move their car, which was blocking the exit of a parking lot. Their reason: they didn't like being told what to do.

In a Midwestern city a group of teen-agers shot out a system of power lines, plunging the city into darkness. Their alibi: they were "bored" and didn't know what to do about it.

In New York, Oakland, Los Angeles, and other cities high school youths terrorize the halls, attacking teachers and other students. Their reason: "prejudice."

On high school and college campuses across the country students picket, march, and demonstrate. Their "causes" vary, but the tenor is always the same: discontent, anger, protest.

The FBI notes that juvenile delinquency is rising at a much more rapid rate than the growth of the population. Worried police officials note an even more alarming statistic: attacks on police officers are mounting, and cooperation with all branches of law enforcement is decreasing.

The slick-magazine writers are kept busy explaining how all this came to be, and "Dear Abby" devotes as much space to parent-child problems as to advice to the lovelorn.

It is our thesis that the whole adolescent generation is at war with adults, not just an extremist group of delinquents. However, it is becoming apparent that the age at which our young people are turning to delinquency is *decreasing*. We are also becoming aware of perhaps another even more distressing phenomenon—that these acts of violence and destruction are not confined to those children ordinarily considered as coming from "across the tracks" but are being manifested among all social and economic segments of our society. At this point no home in America can be considered exempt.

No parent today can safely feel that none of his children might become one of these vandals.

We are becoming aware that the attitudes of today's children, regardless of age, are quite different from what they were in "the good old days." Children no longer accept parents' judgments as absolute. Indeed, in many cases they pay little attention to them at all. Parents are called upon to justify their actions in ways which were not expected of them in the past. In addition, defiance and even outright rebellion are becoming more characteristic of even very small children. Fifty or even thirty years ago no child would dream of "getting the law" on his parents after he had been beaten by his father. Today this is a relatively commonplace occurrence. In more than one instance we have read where children have shot and killed their parents for some real or fancied grievance that they held. Far more frequent are the covert or hidden manifestations of this rebellion, the *unwillingness* rather than the inability of children to learn, to function, and to cooperate in the school and at home.

As has been mentioned, of course, the extreme manifestation of this is in the behavior of teen-agers. Though generally unrecognized as yet by the community at large, the growing acts of juvenile delinquency represent little less than outright warfare between some adolescents and society. It has been suggested that the basis for this warfare is far more profound than has been previously assumed, and that, in reality, the whole adolescent generation is at war with adults. Perhaps even more than this, adolescents resent the unwillingness of the adult community to give them any part in deciding about activities and regulations regarding their own welfare. Perhaps the only hopeful sign in the picture at present is that more and more young people are joining the constructive movements which are working to shape our country's future. The Peace Corps and some of the groups attempting to achieve racial equality in this country are perhaps the best examples of this. At least some young people are finding fulfillment in the kind of creative and cooperative activity which is the best counteraction for the poisons which have led to the war between the generations.

At the same time, however, another movement is also growing at an alarmingly rapid rate and recruiting many of our young people in its ranks. Though often young people may be able to channel their hostilities and desires to rebel against authority in a relatively constructive direction, such as in some of the nonviolent movements, all too often they are taken in by the openly antisocial groups and thus further directed away from achieving status in the community. There are those who contend that today's rebels are an inevitable by-product of the democratic process; but their number and activities are increasing at a rate that leaves us little room for complacency. The attitude of throwing up one's hands is also becoming more prevalent in this area, as well as in adult-child relationships, when we attempt to deal with the problem.

UNDERLYING SOURCES OF THE PROBLEM

Numerous theories have been advanced to attempt to explain some of the facts that have been presented. One psychoanalytic writer, in commenting on the vandalism committed by the young socialites at the party mentioned previously, called the act the result of "mass psychosis." He suggested that their underlying need was "to be punished," because they felt that their parents had not been firm enough with them as young children. Another writer suggested that these children suffered from what he calls "anomie"—the feeling of rootlessness, of being cut off or not belonging to other members of society. Still others have suggested that in this materialistic age children are suffering from what is called decay in moral and spiritual values. Perhaps there is an element of truth in all these statements, but they appear to suffer from the shortcomings that characterize most theories of this sort. Either the theorists are attempting to treat only symptoms, or their concepts are so vague and general as to have little specific bearing on the situation confronting us. They appear also to have little understanding of the forces and events which are shaping the world of today and tomorrow.

The factor which would seem to underlie the whole scope of these problems is the rapid and overwhelming social upheaval which is taking place in our current era. The first of such changes occurred some eight to ten thousand years ago when primitive man started to break the tribal chains and establish the beginnings of modern civilization.

Primitive society, which was relatively homogenous, gave way to the caste and class system of civilization.

The early myths and tales of all civilized peoples include stories of man in revolt—against his gods, his rulers, his competitors. Adam, Cain, and Prometheus rebelled—and suffered accordingly; so did Brunhild, Medea, and Antigone on the female side.

Thus civilization has been consistently the revolt of one group displacing its former rulers and leading to a new order and a new rebellion. The world has been a long time "going to the dogs." Why is the current trend more acute and more dangerous?

Today, with the advent of democracy, the previously suppressed can openly rebel; women, the colored races, labor, the poor, and children openly rebel against authoritarian domination. In a democracy each individual can no longer be denied or deprived of his dignity and value. Man is no longer willing to be an insignificant particle of a mass.

Old-style authoritarianism still exists. Two fifths of the world's peoples still live under some sort of dictatorship. But resistance is building up to the old and new forms of domination, and that resistance follows similar tactics wherever the suppressed, neglected, or disrespected claim their equal right and value.

There is a similar desire behind all forms of revolts: to be recognized as an equal. This is what Alfred Adler[1] formulated as possibly the first social law—the law of equality, the ironclad logic of social living which demands recognition of every human being as an equal.

THE PARENTS' DILEMMA

In our present situation parents are confronted by what seems to be a hopelessly unresolvable conflict. On the one hand they are exhorted by newspaper articles, by judges, by police, and by school officials to "keep their children in line"; on the other hand they see themselves as being unable to cope with the rebellious behavior of most children by the methods that they have learned from the past. In no area is this more clearly shown than in the legal requirement that parents are responsible for the acts of their children until they reach at least age eighteen and in some cases until they reach age twenty-one. Often the judge in remanding a juvenile offender to the custody of his parents sternly admonishes them to see to it that "this doesn't happen again"; yet he rarely gives them any useful advice on prevention. If he does offer advice it is usually of the "go-to-the-woodshed" brand, but he does not tell the parent how to go about spanking a child who is as big or bigger physically than the parent.

At the same time the parent may also be in trouble with the law if he is *too* severe with his children. As many parents have realized, it is physically impossible for them to prevent an adolescent from leaving home at any hour he chooses or indulging in any misbehavior within his physical capacity and circumstance. The same can be said of many younger children, except that their range of operation may be somewhat limited by the fact that they do not know how to drive a car. But as most of us are aware, vandalism today is not by any means confined to teen-agers or older individuals. It is little wonder that parents today feel so frustrated when cajoling, bribing, scolding, restricting of privileges, and even beating fail to achieve the desired result.

Parental frustration is increased further by the Freudian dictum which has haunted a whole generation of parents: "You have got to love your child or else something is wrong with you." (Conversely, if you love your

---

[1] Alfred Adler, *Social Interest: A Challenge to Mankind.* London, Faber & Faber, 1938.

children, nothing else matters.) Coupled with this is the warning that a child must be allowed to express his feelings or else he will grow up to be guilt-ridden and full of inhibitions. Though there is little doubt that Freud's original concepts have been misapplied, if one were to predict the logical result of such upbringing, it is not hard to see why so many of our educated, middle-class children are, in the name of equality, living in flophouses, sniffing glue, or busily engaged in denying political candidates with whom they disagree even the basic right to speak.

However, it is our feeling that the roots of this problem lie much deeper. It would not be difficult to see that these Freudian concepts have hardly been adopted by lower-class or particularly ghetto parents. Among their children the rebelliousness, the militancy, and the demands for rights seem to be even more prevalent and have, perhaps, a much more realistic base. But what most parents must recognize is that the keynote of this troublesome age everywhere is *equality and freedom,* and the rights children are demanding today are those which are being sought by all other groups in our society. At the same time this is not an isolated phenomenon but one which is being manifested all over the world, even in countries with dictatorships. One result of this is that parents have been literally forced into giving children more freedom, but they have not been able to teach children how to use this right of freedom sensibly. Perhaps this is because in earlier days the father was the boss in the family and although the mother and children often did not like what he said or did, at least they knew where the source of authority was. By accepting this authority they managed to feel reasonably secure. Unfortunately, all too many of our homes today are full of potential bosses, each of whom is attempting to exert his right to do as he pleases regardless of whether it interferes with the rights of others. This of course is not freedom but anarchy. Unless there is respect for the rights of others and the understanding that no one is really the boss in today's family, there is not true democracy but chaos. When parents begin to understand that though they cannot stop a child from doing whatever his physical capacity will let him do, they *can* teach him that every act has a consequence for which he is responsible, then perhaps we will be able to live together as equals.

"WE WANT MORE TO SAY"

Another distressing by-product of the misunderstanding between generations is that parents, in their efforts to use the outmoded, autocratic methods of discipline to control their children, still deny them one of the rights that is indispensable to equality: a say in their own affairs. Much of the rebelliousness of young people today against the established order seems to stem from this lack rather than from one of the others previously discussed. Children see around them other previously disfranchised groups gaining more and more rights and having more and more to say about the management of their own affairs. Women, workers, and minority groups are demanding, and to a considerable extent getting, the right to participate in the democratic process, but we are paying only lip service to that demand from children. One has merely to look at the sorry state of student government in our schools to see that this is true. Students who do run for school offices go through all the motions of democracy but are not allowed to make any of the vital decisions; consequently they become scornful, apathetic, or in increasing numbers turn to less acceptable ways of being heard.

So it appears quite obvious that a new tradition in child rearing is needed, one that will not only fulfill this need for children to learn how to manage their own affairs and participate in the democratic process, but will help all of us to deal more effectively with the social revolution we find going on around us.

CHAPTER 2

UNDERSTANDING THE CHILD'S PERSONALITY

It is a truism that it is necessary to understand the child before one can deal with him. Today's parents are deluged with advice from many sources on how to raise their children. Most of this is in the form of prescriptions— what to do or not to do when the child behaves a certain way in a given circumstance—but little information is given to parents on how to understand children. Some so-called experts believe the human personality is so complex that only a trained psychologist or psychiatrist can understand it; others believe personality can be manipulated in any chosen direction by the "proven" use of rewards and punishments. But what is crucial here is that every individual is unique and different from every other individual. Though most research done on behavior is devoted to finding out in what ways human beings are alike, the truth is that we are both different and alike, that we all have certain fundamental human needs in common, but that each of us interprets and deals with these needs and goals somewhat differently. It is our belief that understanding just a few of the more important ways in which we are alike will aid parents greatly in better understanding their children. These principles are derived in whole or in part from the theories of Alfred Adler. In a sense they provide a basic framework for the concepts and techniques described in this book.

THE NEED TO BELONG

The threat of being rejected by others is perhaps the greatest fear any person can experience. Adults learn to hide the consequences of possible rejection by others in a bewildering variety of ways which Freud called "mechanisms." On the other hand we often misinterpret a situation to mean that we are being rejected when in truth we are not. Although children may try to hide their real feelings from us, we can fairly easily tell by their actions whether or not they feel accepted.

AFFECTION, APPROVAL, AND ATTENTION

In today's competitive world the fact that we are dependent upon one another for all the basic needs of life is often quite underrated, but the dependence of an infant child upon his mother is better understood. Without her care, or the care of a mother substitute, the infant would obviously perish in a few hours. There is far more involved than the satisfaction of pure physical need. Research has shown us that without affection and love, and intellectual and physical stimulus from the mother, the child will not develop as a normal human being. But research has also shown that though it is most often the mother who provides this, emotional warmth and stimulation can come from any human being who cares.

What should also be obvious is that the attitudes which come from total dependence on someone else for the vital needs of life are ones which shape the infant's whole development thereafter.

In the first weeks after birth the child responds to what happens to him in terms of what some psychologists have called "mass action." If he is angry or hungry, his face and body turn red, he waves his arms and legs around, and he cries all at the same time. Though a similar process may take place when he is loved or cuddled, it is not very long before he learns to respond differently to loving than to fear or anger. He also learns something more important: mother does not always respond to every demand that he makes with love and satisfaction of his need. Often he finds that his bottle does not come or his diapers are not changed when he desires, but rather at certain prescribed times. Thus the process of training begins.

When the child is learning a set of responses to various acts of the mother, his behavior is still much on a trial-and-error basis. The responses that produce the best results for him are kept, the others are quickly dropped. He also learns quickly that if he cries persistently in a situation, eventually he gets what he wants. In others, crying does not seem to produce results, so is dispensed with as a response.

Parents should also remember that an infant in the first few months of life hears only sounds and can interpret very little of what he sees; thus most of his judgments of parental behavior toward him is on the basis of touch and sound. A child learns quickly by the mother's touch and the sound of her voice whether she is angry, elated, or sad. This ability endures long after language has been developed and bewilders parents greatly. They often forget the years of self-training during which the child learned to interpret their moods without the need of language. The most important lesson to be learned here is that parents who attempt to disguise their true feelings in front of children will usually fail.

As the child develops, he learns that certain acts bring certain responses from his parents. He is also learning to interpret what is happening to him. If there are older children in the family, he begins to compare himself with them and to decide who gets more affection from the parents than he does. It is here that he often begins to mistake approval for affection. Many of his mistakes in interpretation may be the result of traditional methods of punishment. Scolding, isolation, or spanking are often regarded by small children as an absence of parental love. Though as a result of this, small children usually strive to do things which bring favorable attention from the parents, often the parents fail to take advantage of this. In the families of an earlier, less urbanized time, as soon as children were able to walk they were given tasks and chores because their help *was* needed. In today's complex society there is usually not enough work to go around, and mothers and fathers often regard the attempts of little children to help out around the house as more of a nuisance than a benefit, particularly when Jimmy sprays furniture polish on the walls of the house rather than on the furniture. As a result, most small children at one time or another come to the conclusion that if they cannot get affection or approval, at least they can get attention. And if they cannot get favorable attention, they will settle for unfavorable attention because their greatest fear is to be ignored.

THE FAMILY CONSTELLATION

It may come as a surprise to many parents to realize that personality differences between siblings are more often the result of their competitive striving than of heredity or other factors. How many times have parents said or thought to themselves, "Why doesn't Joe do as well in school as Jim? The counselors at school say he is just as bright as Jim, but he doesn't seem to care about schoolwork—all he wants to do is play around with cars or go surfing." What they fail to realize is that Jim's academic prowess is precisely the reason why Joe is uninterested in scholarship. When the oldest child achieves competence in a certain area, the second child will rarely attempt to rival him in this area unless he feels he can overtake him or become better.

If Joe had been a girl, the result might have been different, because until puberty, girls generally tend to be somewhat more mature physically and intellectually than boys their same age. Let us say Joe, who is one year younger than Jim, has become Jane. Somewhere in her early school development Jane realizes that she *can* do better at school than Jim. If she succeeds, then Jim may suddenly lose interest in academic pursuits and turn to athletics or mechanical pursuits where he is unlikely to have competition from Jane.

Another factor here is the *cultural* expectation: though many of our teenagers, young adults, and most certainly the fashion designers are busily engaged in attempting to eliminate sexual differences between men and women, most middle-class parents still expect boys to be rough and tough and dirty, to be physically more active and mentally more mischievous than girls. Girls are supposed to be neat and well-behaved, to like studying and books, and to misbehave rarely. Unfortunately, somewhere along the line boys are expected to abandon all this and become engineers, physicists, and doctors; girls are expected to study hard, get a college education, and then then get married and raise babies. It is not surprising to see that such conflicts in the expectations of parents make it difficult for boys and girls to establish their identities during adolescence and even as young adults. What must be remembered is the principle mentioned above: when one child stakes out an area of competency for himself, the younger child will rarely challenge this, but will go in a different direction, often the opposite. This is purposive behavior, though the child is not aware of the motives behind his behavior. If the oldest child happens to be a girl who follows the expectancy of middle-class parents, she becomes responsible, good, and academic. If the second child is a boy who feels sufficiently discouraged about getting favorable recognition from his parents, he may decide to be just the opposite of his sister—irresponsible, bad, and not studious. Of course parents must remember that each child interprets his situation somewhat differently from any other child. However, there are certain facts and principles which parents need to understand in order to know their children better.

THE CHILD'S POSITION IN THE FAMILY

One might argue that each child's position in the family is unique; nevertheless, the effect of position on the child's development has been greatly underestimated. Naturally, position is influenced by factors such as sex of the child, the distances in age between children in a given family, how the parents deal with the children. But in order for parents to understand better what happens, the *facts* which are present in each situation deserve analysis.

THE OLDEST CHILD

The most obvious fact for the oldest child is that for a time he is the only child for his parents' attention. Then he is displaced, or "dethroned," as Adler described it. How traumatic this displacement is for the oldest child varies from family to family, depending on how many years later the second child is born and the maturity with which the parents deal with the situation. But it is reasonable to assume that if the age differential is five years or less, the shock is rather extreme. Even at age five, when the child's style of life is well developed, it is difficult to impart to him that the need by the parents to spend more time in caring for the new arrival does not necessarily mean rejection of *him*. If the age difference is three years or less, there is no way to explain this to the child; the only way to compensate for loss is to give the child extra attention. This extra attention may come as the result of displays of temper or various negative ways by which the child attempts to make his presence known. All too often if the parents fall into this trap, the stage is set for more serious disturbances to follow.

The second fact for the oldest child is the parents' lack of experience in dealing with their first child. There is probably greater variation in the effects of this than in the case of displacement. In general, parents are more anxious, more overprotective, and more indulgent than they are with later children. Perhaps the best example of this is in the baby book: for the first child every step, every landmark, every tooth, every stage of development is lovingly recorded, often documented with pictures and drawings. In some instances the second child may get a page or two, but the third child is lucky if his name is recorded in the book.

Though it is rather obvious that most oldest children overcome these traumas satisfactorily, research has indicated that certain personality characteristics are more common among first and second children in families where the age differential is less than five or six years—which probably would include most families in this country. Oldest children tend to be more conservative, to prefer authority (particularly their own), to dislike change, but they are better administrators and managers than second children, largely because parents tend to invest the oldest child with more responsibility. This is a tradition that goes back to earlier days when, particularly in rural families, every pair of hands was needed to help harvest the crops or maintain the household; particularly, the firstborn son was expected to assume the mantle of responsibility and ultimately the control of the family fortunes. And the older girls who may have preceded him were not denied their share of the work—only the authority that went with masculine prerogatives. In our contemporary society this responsibility, and to some degree the authority that goes with it, seems more often to end up in the hands of the first child.

THE SECOND CHILD

It should not be difficult to see how opposites of personality and development tend to appear with the first and second child. The most important fact confronting the second child is that he usually has someone older, larger, and more capable ahead of him. (There are exceptions. The first child may be handicapped by illness, or if the two children are very close together in age, the second may mature more rapidly, physically and mentally, and overtake the first child.) In most cases the second child sees the first as what Adler called a "pacemaker," and his goal is to overtake and supplant the first child in the attention and affection of the parents. With the benefit of added experience, parents are usually less inclined to make many of the mistakes they made with the first child. Research has indicated that the second child is generally much more flexible than the first, sees change as a means of gaining power, is more apt to be creative, but is less consistent in carrying out his ideas than the first child. If there are no further children, the second child has the added advantage of never being displaced. It is not hard to see why research has indicated that of all the positions, the oldest seems a little more prone to behavior and personality difficulties than do children in the other positions. Although most oldest children make a satisfactory adjustment, a slightly disproportionate number of oldest children are apt to be involved in delinquent behavior or among those who seek help at guidance clinics or mental hospitals.

THE MIDDLE CHILD

If a third child arrives in the family, obviously displacement must be added to the problems faced by the second child. Generally, he finds it necessary not only to compete in one area with a sibling who is larger and stronger and more capable than he is, but to share his attention and affection with the new arrival. If he is not able to react positively to this, he often finds himself vacillating between the desire to be responsible like the oldest child or to be a baby like the youngest. If he is not able to overcome this successfully, the middle child often finds himself unable to develop a true identity.

THE YOUNGEST CHILD

The youngest child, of course, enjoys one unique advantage not shared by the children ahead of him. He is never displaced. The larger the family, the more apt he is to find himself in the enviable position of being the baby with a whole host of mammas and papas eager to gain parental approval by babying him. Despite the fact that youngest children are more often spoiled than those in other positions, they seem to be the ones who react the least unfavorably to being spoiled. It is also interesting to note that whenever a break in the family pattern occurs, the youngest seems to be the one most likely to choose an occupation or avocation where his personality characteristics or activities run counter to the prevailing family pattern.

THE ONLY CHILD

Though the only child enjoys the advantage of not being displaced, this is often counteracted by the fact that he has no one close to him in age or capability and must therefore orient himself entirely to the parents. Often this results in a competition between the members of the family of the same sex for the approval or favorable attention of the parent of the opposite sex. Though it usually takes the only child longer to develop the ability to relate socially with his peers, this does not appear to affect significantly his ability to adjust to the world as an adult.

LARGE FAMILIES

Because of the relative stability and similarity of the five clear-cut positions mentioned above, generalizations derived from research findings and observations of children in these positions are feasible. However, in large families the middle children who are between the oldest children and the youngest do not necessarily follow consistent behavioral trends in their development. The factors of age distances, sex, parental behavior, and family circumstances affect middle children differently. Most important, parents of many children should notice how any given child reacts to the children closest to him in age, whether older or younger.

THE ROLE OF THE PARENTS

As can be easily understood, the way parents react to these situations is of crucial importance. In dealing with their children, parents must see to it that each child is encouraged in some positive or cooperative direction which is independent of those taken by the other children in the family. Because of their own ambitions for the children, parents often fail to see the value of any activities which can be useful and satisfying to their children, but which do not fit their own particular standards. For example, parents with high academic aspirations for their children are often upset over the failure of a second child to repeat the academic prowess of the first. They do not understand that the second child is unwilling to compete in any area which he feels is dominated by the first child. Therefore his choice is in a different, often opposite, direction. Any attempt by the parent to push the second child in the direction of the first is almost inevitably met with great resistance. "Why can't you be a good student like your sister?" is the frequent lament of frustrated parents who put their own ambitions for a child ahead of his self-interest. If the first child is academic, it is the wise parent who encourages the second child in any useful activity he likes, whether it is mechanical, athletic, or social. Parents are often mystified to discover that when the first child has finished school and left home, the second child, who has been noticeably indifferent to his studies, all of a sudden becomes an academic wizard. Parents who understand the dynamics behind this behavior will see it as being purposive, though the child is not aware of the true nature of his goal.

The major danger facing parents if they are unwilling or unable to understand the inclinations of their children is that one child may decide he cannot get recognition through positive competition with his brothers or sisters, but he can gain a great deal of attention by going in the opposite direction. He then becomes what is aptly termed "the best worst": if he is lazy, irresponsible, disruptive, or does poor work at school, one can be sure that this will call down upon him scoldings, punishments, and admonitions to do better, as well as parental despair, which is exactly what he wants. Every effort to "make" him improve is met with more resistance. The tragedy is that often children train themselves in these habits to the degree that when the need for this kind of attention is gone, they have not learned to function in any other way.

The same characteristics develop in the various positions in deprived homes, but the ground rules are not the same. Because of their own discouragement in facing a hostile and indifferent world, parents are either unable or unwilling to provide any kind of encouragement for children who seek to be constructive. As a result, the children are left pretty much on their own, and only extreme behavior like fighting, vandalism, and destructiveness is enough to get the parents' attention. In school such a child feels lost; he sees no value in learning. He is usually confronted with a succession of failures from the minute he enters school and he either drops out or "sits" out his term. Violence, sex, and drugs seem to be the only answer to this kind of discouragement.

THE MISTAKEN GOALS OF BEHAVIOR

There was a time when there were many opportunities for children to get recognition through constructive means. Because there were fewer labor-saving devices, parents needed much more help in operating the household; thus children were called upon for a great variety of tasks. Children not only felt the responsibility that went with participation in the family group, but they felt more needed and more sure of their place in the family. Today, particularly in middle- or upper-class homes, parents have to "make" work available for children. Often the children resent the contrived way in which these tasks are imposed. As a result, it is not difficult to see why children use negative, rebellious ways to gain recognition. However, if parents can learn to identify the reasons behind misbehavior and understand it, they are in a better position to correct it.

All misbehavior is the result of a child's mistaken assumption about the way to find a place and gain status. When the adult is not aware of the meaning of the child's misbehavior, he responds by falling for the child's unconscious scheme and reinforces the child's mistaken goal. In order to deal more effectively with the child in the situation, the adult must recognize misbehavior patterns and their hidden goals. We have identified four such goals: (1) attention getting, (2) the struggle for power, (3) revenge, and (4) using disability as an excuse.

1. Attention getting

Mother was in the kitchen finishing up the breakfast dishes when she heard a familiar sound. Jimmy, age 3, came running into the kitchen sobbing, "He hit me, he hit me." Wearily, mother left her dishes and went to investigate. Jimmy followed behind, still crying lustily. Bobby, age 5, was in his room playing with his crayon book. "Now what happened?" mother said exasperatedly. "Did you hit Jimmy?" "Mother, he took my crayons and I told him he couldn't play with my crayons." "That's no excuse for you to hit him," said mother. "For that you have to stay in your room for an hour." "But that's not fair, it was his fault." Bobby started to cry. Mother left the room, a triumphant Jimmy behind her. Ten minutes later they were at it again.

How often is this scene repeated in homes all over America. But the mother does not often understand that the *purpose* of her children's fighting is to get her to intervene, to take sides, to scold or punish one or both children. Her intervention in the squabble, however fair she may feel she is in adjudicating the issue, is reinforcing the children's desire for attention. Regardless of the result, except in cases where a severely disturbed older child might injure a younger child, the wisest course for the mother is to let the children themselves settle the matter. When they discover that mother will not intervene in a fight, it usually stops. Of course getting attention is not confined to the behavior of children. In one or more forms this behavior can be observed in most adults.

Getting attention is more often identified with disturbed behavior, but behind the cooperative behavior of very young children may also be the desire for special attention. In fact it is often extremely difficult to distinguish between behavior for the sake of attention getting and cooperative behavior which stems from a genuine feeling of belongingness and willingness to contribute. Generally speaking, however, the "successful" child whose goal in attention getting is to be the best or better than the other children is often a perfectionist, very sensitive to criticism and fearful of failure. He needs to realize that constant testimonials are unnecessary to prove his value and that satisfaction is inherent in the cooperative activity itself rather than in the favorable response it provokes.

There are innumerable manifestations of negative, attention-getting behavior. A child may be always "getting into things," failing to do his chores, fighting with his brothers and sisters. He may be a dawdler, unable to dress or occupy himself. But what is important for parents to understand is that the desire underlying these acts is to get adults to pay attention to him and to serve him. Later in this book methods on how to deal with the problem will be discussed.

2. *The struggle for power*

"Joe, I told you an hour ago to mow the lawn." Father's voice was insistent, irritated. "All right, all right, but I was busy in my room." "I don't want to hear another word out of you. Go out and mow the lawn immediately." "All right, all right, in a minute." Five minutes later father poked his head out of the door. "Joe, I thought I told you to mow the lawn. Where are you, Joe?" A voice answered from the garage, "I'll be there in a minute. I'm just finding an oil can to oil the lawn mower." "Now you get here this minute or you'll get no allowance for another week."

Although in this case the boy is only skirting the edges of open defiance, the father does not realize that the child's motive is power. What most parents do not know is that the child's goal is *to get the parent involved in the struggle*, not necessarily to win it. Of course the boy would like to avoid mowing the lawn; he views household chores as distasteful, largely because he has little say about which chores he might prefer over others —or whether he should do them at all. Regardless of the end results, getting his father involved in the struggle serves his purpose. What he is really doing is making the parent dance to his tune by trying to force him to do something which he does not want to do. The same thing happens when a parent attempts to correct misbehavior which may have originally been for attention only; a refusal by the child to stop nearly always forces a parent to more punitive behavior in order to reassert the control he thinks he has lost. While the child often ultimately does not win such a struggle, he secures a "victory" each time he can defeat an order or a command. Thus the parent who allows himself to get into an argument with a child, trying to force compliance of his demands, experiences endless "defeats"; in fact he is actually playing into the child's hands. *Once the battle has been joined, the child has already won it!*

3. *Revenge*

Three teen-agers were driving in a battered old car along a fairly empty street when they saw an old man shuffling along the sidewalk. One boy said to the others, "Let's try him." Though the old man pitifully asserted that he had no money and nothing to give them, the three boys beat him until he was senseless and bleeding in the road. Then they jumped into their car and drove away.

Most middle-class adults are horrified when hearing or reading about such a crime. The newspapers label it "senseless" or "motiveless." In truth, there is no such thing as a motiveless act; there is a purpose behind every behavior. In this case the old man was merely an innocent victim of three boys taking out their hatred and revenge on a society in which they feel they have no place, on a person who is weaker than they are and therefore less able to resist.

The child whose behavior is motivated by revenge displays a disturbance which borders on the pathologic. Generally this goal is sought only after a long series of discouragements where the child has decided that attention getting and power will not compensate him for his utter lack of a sense of belonging. The child bent on revenge has given up hope of attaining any worthiness through constructive activities. He has reached the stage where he thinks everybody is against him, and the only way to get recognition is to retaliate against adults for the way he feels he has been treated. Usually he is right in his interpretation; he *has been* pushed around. He just does not realize how his offensive behavior almost compels the kind of treatment he has received.

The behavior of most delinquent children is an expression of revenge. Generally they feel that the only way to be recognized is to provoke hostility. This leads to punishment by society, which in turn provokes further hostility by the delinquent. The end result of this unhappy cycle is all too often the habitual criminal who feels the urge to commit more crimes as soon as he is released from prison. He is fighting a war with society and he is willing to accept the fortunes of this war. Parents who have such children often throw up their hands in despair. If a delinquent child has reached adolescence there is little a parent can do without professional help, though the parent can learn to change his own behavior so as not to respond to the old provocations. If he is at all successful, sometimes a communication can be reestablished with the child. Generally speaking, the only way a child in revenge can be helped is by convincing him that you, at least, are not going to act toward him the way he feels everyone else is. If you can do this, there is sometimes hope of saving him before it is too late.

4. Using disability as an excuse

"But Sally, why can't you get those problems right?" mother asked. "After all, you do well in reading and writing; why can't you do those arithmetic problems?" "I told you, I'm just dumb in arithmetic," Sally cried. "My teacher thinks so too." "Has she said anything like this?" mother demanded. "No, but she only answers the questions of the bright kids. I tell you, I'm just dumb in mathematics." "Oh, I guess you're right," the mother sighed. "Your father and I were never very good in mathematics either. It must run in the family."

Parents are unusually willing to accept a child's expressions of defeat in areas where they themselves have had trouble. What they fail to see is that the lack of ability is *assumed* by the child rather than real. This is perhaps where the most extreme form of discouragement is manifested. The child has given up making any effort; he wants little more than to be left alone so that his deficiency may not be so painfully obvious. What is surprising is how often we find relatively well-functioning individuals who assume disabilities in specific areas though not as total failures. An assumed inadequacy in mathematics is probably one of the most common forms of this. A child who functions up to grade level or above in the verbal areas should ordinarily be able to do as well in mathematics. If he does not, it is because he is psychologically discouraged. However, he has another motive: that is to invite discouragement and despair on the part of the parents and teachers who try to help him (usually he has little trouble in being successful at this). On the other hand, regardless of how parents feel, they should avoid at all costs pushing or pressuring the child to succeed in areas where he feels inadequate. Rather they should stimulate and encourage him in areas where he does feel successful. In this way he might one day be willing to risk a failure in mathematics should he find a practical need for competence in this skill.

We are also concerned with children whose assumed disability or inadequacy is a total behavior pattern. Recent research findings have supported the attitude that we have held for many years, that is, that the great majority of deficiencies of functioning, particularly in the intellectual areas, are the result of discouragement, not of any innate inability. In other words, with the exception of children with known neurological or physical defects, mental retardation is primarily a psychological deficiency in earlier years. However, there is some evidence also to support the idea that if the right kind of stimulation is not given to the child by the time he reaches nine or ten years of age, he may not be able to improve his ability thereafter.

The important thing here is that if the child feels inadequate and incapable of functioning, he will not try, whether or not his deficiency is assumed or real. Only very recently have we become aware of the devastating effect our present educational system of standards and grades has in discouraging countless numbers of children, regardless of their socioeconomic level, from attempting to learn. In the case of the ghetto child, he is often totally unable to communicate with a middle-class teacher without special help. The results are no less devastating for a child from a more favored home who falls behind for a variety of reasons but who uses his disability as an excuse to gain sympathy and attention from his parents and teachers.

Perhaps one of the most common forms of this assumed disability is in reading retardation. With all the bewildering array of researches, theories, and concepts regarding the nature of reading retardation, investigators have never been able to come up with a satisfactory explanation of why *more than 75 percent of all retarded readers are boys.* There is no evidence to support any visual, motor, or intellectual inferiority of boys over girls. Then what is the answer? Perhaps the researchers could look at the cultural imperative which dictates that girls are expected to like books and reading but boys are not, at least not until high school. Also, anywhere except in deprived neighborhoods, falling behind in reading brings an inordinate amount of special attention from parents, teachers, and the community. Often the disability may have started as the result of some real difficulty the child encountered, but he quickly realized that it is a most effective way of keeping his parents involved with him. Thus the motive is built in to continue the disability even when no longer necessary.

Perhaps one of the most important, and most difficult, recommendations that parents should follow in the situation of reading deficiencies is to *leave any type of special training in the hands of the school.* Parents themselves should never try to tutor their child in the disability, even if the school recommends such special help. If the problem is severe enough, the child should be referred to a special clinic that deals with such disorders. If the problem is less severe but special help is still needed, it can be provided by an older child who is not a member of the family. Parents should remain noncommittal regardless of their true feelings. In this way they avoid reinforcing the child's attempt to use the disability as a means of getting recognition from them and thus leaving him free to find the answer on his own, whether he wants to improve or not. Often when the child realizes he is free to make this decision, his recovery can be dramatically swift.

THE IMPORTANCE OF EXPECTANCY

Underlying all the interactions previously described are the expectations of the child. Every child—or adult for that matter—acts according to the way he expects things to happen. Most parents respond to the child's expectations and in that way reinforce his behavior. Thus if a child who repeatedly acts up at dinner is scolded and told to be quiet, this procedure reinforces his behavior method instead of teaching him to behave differently in the future. Similarly the revengeful child who provokes hostility does so because he wants and expects abuse so he can feel justified in what he does. In other words, in order to understand the child's actions, one has to see them whole, not as emanating solely from the child, but as being part of the total situation in which the child, his peers, his parents, and his teachers all cooperate to give meaning to what he does, whether it is right or wrong.

CHAPTER 3

PRINCIPLES INVOLVED
IN THE NEW TRADITION

Raising children has always been based on tradition, but few people realize the cultural abnormality of our times. No other species on this earth besides this generation of adults needed lectures, books, and instruction about what to do with their young. Each generation learned it from the previous one. Margaret Mead [1] described a number of primitive societies, each of which raised children in different ways and brought about the development of specific personality types; but in each tribe children were probably raised in the same way for thousands of generations, and each adult and each child knew what to do in certain complex situations. It was the advent of democracy which caused the present dilemma. In ancient Rome and Greece, Cicero and Plato complained about the children's lack of respect for their elders. A similar democratic period in the last few centuries caused changes in human relationships and created educational difficulties. In the democratic evolution, with its increased degree of equality, each new generation of children gained more freedom and challenged to an increasingly successful degree the authority of elders. Today we can no longer "make" the child behave, study, or apply himself.

Pressure from without has lost effectiveness as a method for dealing with children. Reward and punishment were useful in an autocratic setting, but today if we give a reward, the child no longer accepts it gratefully as a favor of a benevolent authority; no, he regards it as his *right*, and he will not do anything unless another reward is forthcoming. The situation is worse in regard to punishment. The only children who respond well to punishment are those who do not need it, with whom one can reason. Those whom we try to impress with punitive consequences may respond briefly, and then resume their defiance. They feel that if the adult has the right to punish, they have the same right too. Mutual retaliations fill our homes and schools. The first step toward a new educational policy must be the realization that one cannot hope for good results through punishment. It has to be replaced by the application of logical or natural consequences where the child is impressed with the needs of reality, not with the power of adults.

[1] Margaret Mead, *From the South Seas.* New York, William Morrow, 1939.

STIMULATION INSTEAD OF PRESSURE

The traditional autocratic approach of motivating children through pressure from without must be replaced with stimulation from within. Parents and teacher alike must become familiar with new methods, which are new only in the sense that they are generally unknown, although educators for decades have been promoting similar approaches. The basic principle is to deal with each other as equals, to establish a relationship based on mutual respect. Our children have become our equals, not in size, skill, and experience, but in their right and ability to decide for themselves instead of yielding to a superior power. Most mistakes with children stem from the lack of mutual respect needed in dealing with equals.

Conflicts of interest and desire always exist when people live together. In the past such conflicts were resolved by the stronger person; the weaker had merely to submit. Today such simple solutions of conflicts are no longer effective. The loser immediately challenges—often successfully—the decision imposed upon him. When parents have a conflict with the child, they usually proceed to fight or give in. If they fight, they violate the respect for the child; if they give in, they neglect respect for themselves. But most of us do not know what else to do.

This is the main problem of the emerging new tradition in dealing with children: how not to fight without giving in. It is possible if one becomes familiar with the many ways by which children can be stimulated to meet the needs of the situation, if one is willing to resolve conflicts through agreement. The best formula for children is to treat them with kindness and with firmness. Kindness expresses respect for the child and firmness evokes respect from the child. There are people who are kind but not firm, and others who are firm but not kind. Many are firm and kind, but seldom at the same time.

TECHNIQUES VERSUS ATTITUDES

Parents ask more and more for help in their task of influencing children. They want to know what they should do. They are sincere in this inquiry, but they are seldom given an answer. Many of those who are consulted really do not know what to advise, or they consider giving advice improper. They maintain that any parent who is mature, emotionally stable, and who has the correct attitude toward children does not need any advice; other parents are incapable of benefiting from advice. Consequently, we find the literature filled with generalities, which are often erroneous or without any practical value. Telling a mother that her difficulties with her child are the consequence of her lack of love is, in most cases, an unwarranted insult and not even correct. The mother may have a deep love for her child, but if she does not know what to do with him and feels constantly defeated, she may be so upset that she cannot show her love. What is worse, the desire to show love induces many mothers to spoil their child. All generalities like the advice to have more patience, to give more love and security, are usually meaningless because the parents don't know how to be more patient and give more love.

The proper attitude of a parent is not a *premise* for being effective, but rather its *consequence*. When the mother discovers how she can influence the child and win his cooperation, her attitude begins to change. Then it is not infrequent that the mother for the first time begins to enjoy the child of whom she has been afraid. Few parents today are prepared to deal with the child as an equal. They need information about the methods which are effective in a democratic setting. *Every* mother and father can learn what to do if they want to badly enough, regardless of how disturbed they may be. Our recommendations are so specific that anyone who has the desire to test them can acquire the skill and can learn to apply the techniques. In this regard our approach is often in contrast to prevalent forms of advice and counseling.

The principles for exerting beneficial and corrective influences on the child are the same for parents and for teachers. And yet each has different opportunities. We constantly encounter the question as to whose obligation it is to improve the child's deficiencies and maladjustments. It is characteristic of our time, with its cultural ignorance about educational effectiveness, that each group blames the other for the child's shortcomings and requests the other to correct them. We find this typical situation between father and mother. The less the mother knows what to do with the child, the better she knows what father should do, and vice versa. Passing the buck is the tacit admission of one's inability to find answers to the child's problems. Actually, anyone who understands the child and can win his cooperation can help him improve and adjust, whether he is a parent, a teacher, a relative, a friend of the family, a minister, a youth leader. Parents certainly have it in their reach to change a child's behavior, particularly if he is young. They can use many approaches which the classroom situation does not permit. On the other hand, the teacher has the great advantage of working with the group, and the group exerts stronger influences on children than any adult. As the authority of adults diminishes, the influence of the peer group increases, particularly when the child reaches adolescence. Because of the inadequate training of our present generation of teachers, few realize a teacher's potential for correcting many of the wrong influences of the home and of the community because she can use the classroom group as a means of helping a child to understand his own needs and problems and to correct them.

CHAPTER 4

PSYCHOLOGICAL METHODS IN DEALING WITH CHILDREN

When considering some of the recommended techniques for dealing with children, it is important to distinguish those which require both an understanding of the child's motivations and the social setting from more general methods which can be applied wherever the situation dictates. Such techniques as disinvolvement, and logical consequences, for example, usually require a good deal more analysis and thinking through than the methods of not talking and avoiding comparisons with children. Accordingly, they are dealt with in more detail. Furthermore, the concept of logical consequences, because of its complexity, is dealt with separately in Chapter 6.

ENCOURAGEMENT

Skill in encouraging children is a prerequisite for any effective correction. In many cases the consequences of the parents' actions will depend largely on their ability to encourage or discourage. If the mother's or father's actions contribute to discouragement of the child, then they have done harm, regardless of how justified and understandable the actions may be. Skill in encouraging requires either an unusual kind of person who can exert an encouraging influence on anyone with whom he comes in contact or the learning of this intricate and complex procedure.

Essentially, encouragement involves the ability to accept the child as worthwhile, regardless of any deficiency, and to assist him in developing his capacities and potentialities. Unfortunately, though the principle of providing encouragement is widely accepted, few understand thoroughly the nature of the process and often discourage without meaning to do so. Specifically, the person who encourages: (1) places value on the child as he is, (2) shows faith in the child and enables him to have faith in himself, (3) sincerely believes in the child's ability and wins his confidence while building his self-respect, (4) recognizes a job "well done" and gives recognition for effort, (5) utilizes the family group to facilitate and enhance the development of the child, (6) integrates the group so that each child can be sure of his place in it, (7) assists in the development of skills sequentially so as to assure success, (8) recognizes and focuses on strengths and assets,

(9) utilizes the interest of the child to energize constructive activity.[1] Encouragement, while not a specific approach, is still a psychological procedure, an application of psychological principles in dealing with the child. It is hard to believe how many parents' behavior is discouraging to small children. Here is an illustration.

> Mother was in a hurry to go to the store and Paul, age 4, was trying to tie his last shoe. Impatiently she stood over him. "Hurry up, Paul, we've got to go to the market." "But Mommy, I can't do it," Paul whined. "But you must try. Hurry up, we've got to get going." Finally in exasperation she leaned down and tied his shoe for him.

Paul feels inefficient and discouraged in competing with mother's miraculous abilities. But he has also learned that if he fumbles long enough, mother will do it for him. At the same time, parents want children to help around the house, but only in areas that support them, not in ways that help the children to develop feelings of competency.

> Carol, age 3, was eager to help mother with the housework. One of the things she delighted in doing was using the spray to clean the windows. This was fine, except mother usually had to come and clean up after her and scold her because she had not done a good job. She tried to use the spray to clean the walls as well, but mother slapped her hands and took away the spray.

It may be hard for some parents to believe that the prejudice adults have toward children's ability is little different than prejudice against races. The essence of this is that we are not willing to give credit for the skills children have, because we are too busy or too concerned about how neat the house is or whether precious dishes are protected. We thwart the child in his efforts to try to learn how to do things for himself. To encourage the child we must allow him to take risks: it is better to have ruined furniture than a ruined child. Sometimes it takes a great deal of courage for a parent to let a child go ahead with a new experience.

> Peter, age 7, had just been given his allowance and wanted to buy a model airplane he had seen at the hobbyshop in a busy shopping center. "I can't take you to the store right now, Peter," mother said. "We'll go tomorrow." "I can go up on my bike, Mother," Peter suggested. "You've never been uptown on your bike, Peter, and you know how much traffic there is," mother replied. "I can take care of myself, Mother. Lots of kids go up there

[1] Don Dinkmeyer and Rudolf Dreikurs, *Encouraging Children to Learn: The Encouragement Process*, Englewood Cliffs, N.J., Prentice-Hall, Inc., 1963.

on their bikes." Mother thought it over for a minute. She pictured the line of bikes she had frequently stumbled over outside the hobbyshop. She also pictured the traffic hazard, then she considered that Peter rode his bike to school every day and handled himself very well. "All right, honey, get your model." Peter dashed joyously out of the house. Mother quieted her uneasy feelings. An hour later Peter dashed back into the house with his package. "See, Mother, I got it." "I'm so pleased, Peter," mother said with a beaming smile, "now you can do your own shopping. Isn't that wonderful." [2]

As this example shows, Peter's mother was willing to take the risk and felt sufficient confidence in the child's ability to let him go. Peter in turn reacted positively to her confidence.

Parents should also praise the child's accomplishments whenever possible, but the praise must be directed toward the task, not the child. It is a mistake to say, "Peter, you were a good boy for doing that," because this is a moral judgment. The child is neither good nor bad, only his actions are. But we should also avoid saying that actions are good or bad; it would be better to say, "I like what you're doing, Peter" or "That is very nice" or "That was a good job" or "You did so much better this time than you did before."

EMPHASIZE THE TASK NOT THE RESULT

Another important factor in the use of praise is to emphasize the task itself rather than the outcome, particularly when a child is young and only beginning to learn. Completing a job is not necessarily the sole criterion for praise. If you do too much of this, the child may get the idea that he will only be praised (i.e., that he will only be worthwhile) when he has finished the job and met your standard. The praise may become a reward, which in a sense is a bribe in reverse: the child will do the task only if he gets the reward in the end. Praising his performance during the task will help to give him the idea that the work itself is worthwhile. Completing the task is important, but if a child can learn that there is value and enjoyment in doing the job, he will be more inspired to try harder and develop himself.

A child needs encouragement as a plant needs water and sunshine. Parents who wish to read further in the methods and uses of encouragement are urged to consult the two sources cited earlier.[3]

---

[2] Rudolf Dreikurs and Vicki Soltz, *Children: The Challenge*. New York, Duell, Sloan & Pearce, 1964, p. 53.

[3] Dinkmeyer and Dreikurs, *op. cit.*; Dreikurs and Soltz, *op. cit.*

AVOID REWARDS AND PUNISHMENTS

There is a peculiar link between encouragement and the use of logical consequences, the method dealt with specifically in Chapter 6. There are many who regard both as nothing but the old principle of reward and punishment. And truly the unskilled parent can use encouragement and logical consequences like reward and punishment, but he will not gain the benefits of either. There is a fundamental difference between reward and encouragement, though they have in common a friendly attitude and there-fore seem identical. The difference is in timing and effect. The reward is usually given to a child for something well done, for some achievement, regardless of how small it may be. Encouragement is given when the child fails. Many assume that encouragement can be provided by making certain the child is successful and then rewarding him. Few realize that success can be most discouraging. First, the child may come to the conclusion that he succeeded once, but he cannot do it again; his recent "success" becomes a threat for his future ability to succeed. Worse, such a procedure conveys to the child an assumption, actually shared by most adults and even peers, that he is worthwhile only when he is successful. This attitude is so widely accepted that its fundamentally discouraging effect is hardly noticed.

Similarly, unskilled educators—parents and teachers alike—are inclined to use "consequences" in the form of a punitive retaliation. Under these circumstances the best possible consequence is turned into an ineffective punishment. The tone of voice alone often distinguishes one from the other.

The adult with his diminished sensitivity may not perceive the difference but the child hears and responds accordingly.

DISINVOLVEMENT

In a conflict situation the parent must withdraw from the conflict since he only increases counteraction through efforts to fight. One must withdraw from the child's provocation but not from the child. The child needs atten-tion and recognition, but not when he tries to gain it through misbehavior and deliberate deficiency. Preaching, explaining, and advising is generally useless since the child probably knows that he is doing wrong. Through disinvolvement one can impress the child with the futility of his disturbing behavior. But in order to be able to use the extremely powerful method of withdrawal, one must first realize the goal of the child, the purpose of his transgression, whether it is the desire to attract attention, to show his power, to hurt and get even, or to display his deficiency in order to be left alone. A temper tantrum becomes meaningless if there is no audience. Fights between children (usually staged for the parents' benefit) are settled fast if the children are left to their own devices.

CHAPTER 5
THE SOCIAL METHODS

There are several important dos and don'ts a parent can virtually memorize in order to be more effective in dealing with children. Once the dos and don'ts are learned, the concept of logical consequences is easier to carry to a successful conclusion.

DO LEARN WHEN NOT TO TALK

An important first step for a mother is to learn to be quiet. Talking is extremely ineffective, usually making the child "mother deaf." One cannot talk the child into taking on responsibility: one must *give* it to him.

DON'T THREATEN THE CHILD

One of the least effective methods in dealing with children is to threaten them with punishment if they refuse to behave. Threats reduce respect for the parent in the child's eyes; not only does the parent fail to be firm and act positively in disciplinary situations but he also reveals his strategy to them. No general can hope to win in the end if he reveals his battle strategy to his adversary. The parent should tell the child *once*, in a firm and friendly voice, what he wants. If there is no response, don't talk any more —act.

DO AVOID COMPETITION BETWEEN CHILDREN

Increasing competition between siblings by treating each one as he "deserves" only intensifies their inclination toward being good or bad. The good child will be good because he wants to be better; the bad child finds his approach gratifying because he gains status and power. Only by treating children as a group and letting them take responsibility for whatever any one of them is doing wrong can adults make children realize that each one *is* his brother's keeper.

DON'T FEEL SORRY FOR THE CHILD

If a child is exposed to unfortunate experiences, it is a natural reaction to feel sorry for him. However, observation shows that the pity and sympathy of well-meaning friends and relatives is often harmful. If one feels sorry for the child, regardless of how justifiable such emotional reaction may be, one teaches the child that he has the right to feel sorry for himself; and nobody is as miserable as one who feels sorry for himself. Besides, the child receives the impression that life owes him something and that he has the right to demand more and more. Such an attitude greatly undermines the child's ability to participate and contribute.

DO AVOID OVERPROTECTING THE CHILD

Overprotection has the same discouraging effect as humiliation; it deprives the child of the experience of his own strength.

DON'T OVEREMPHASIZE CHILDREN'S FEARS

Many parents find it difficult to believe that a child's fears are a means of getting special consideration and service. Fears do not always express a child's insecurity; in fact, the child's fear will vanish when the parents express understanding but no special concern. Likewise, the so-called dependent child usually has no "dependency needs." A dependent child is a tyrant who uses real or assumed weaknesses to put others in his service. He will become independent and self-reliant in a short period of time when the parents, in most cases the mother, stop providing service and assistance.

DO PICK AN AREA TO WORK ON

A common mistake made by parents is to attempt to solve all problems at once. As a result, they find themselves continuously at war with their children. They stand over them, demand, haggle, plead, cajole; and the more they try, the worse the battle gets. The most logical way out of this dilemma is to select one area of behavior and work on that until some success has been achieved. What is most interesting about this technique is that during the process the other areas of conflict seem to take care of themselves. However, it is important *not* to select the area of primary concern. If a parent is most upset because his child fails to keep his room tidy, it is wise to concentrate on the proper use of television or on homework problems. Usually the area where the child "bugs" a parent most is related to the parent's own inner feeling of insecurity; as a result, he may find him-

self unable to be firm and to carry through whatever course of action he
has decided upon. Working in a less critical area is more likely to produce
success.

Once the parent has arrived at a solution to a problem of long standing
through the use of a different technique than has been tried before, the
child may suddenly and miraculously abandon other misbehavior. Again,
this is related to the concept of expectancy. When mother no longer haggles
with, nags, or scolds the child for not cleaning up his room, he will discover
he has no clean clothes to wear and will decide to clean his room himself.
When this happens, a basic change in the relationship occurs. A break in
the expectancy pattern has been achieved, and the child must look for new
ways to be recognized. If the child has been encouraged simultaneously
in positive behavior, he may decide that positive behavior is better and
many negative behaviors will disappear. This is obviously an oversimplifica-
tion and there is no way the parent can anticipate when such a change
might take place. But it does serve to explain the basic principle underlying this and other recommended techniques.

DON'T USE PHYSICAL PUNISHMENT
ANY MORE THAN NECESSARY

How often is it necessary to use physical punishment on children? The
answer is *never*. But why do parents so often fall back on this "tried-and-
true" method when "nothing else works"? The reason may be that momen-
tarily the child is frightened into acquiescence, or at least he stops misbehaving. But most of the time physical punishment intensifies his determination to win in the end; though the parent feels relieved because he has
gotten rid of his anger and frustration, the child feels only anger, humiliation, and revenge. In earlier days when the father was the acknowledged
head of the family, punishment was expected and accepted. Today's children feel they do not need to put up with physical punishment without
retaliation.

In homes where the father is still able to maintain authority by physical
punishment, children do not openly flout his rule. But often in such families
the children will deliberately provoke such punishment in order to be recognized, then in turn will respond subtly by stealing, lying, and bullying
children who are smaller and weaker. These children usually grow up with
the idea that violence is the only logical way to solve problems. In the
ghettos we see some of this pattern, except that the police and the school
are the authority figures instead of the father. As the authoritarian structure
breaks down (and it does even in the ghettos), it is imperative for *all*
parents and teachers to redouble their efforts to teach children that au-

thority comes from within the individual, and that self-discipline in a democracy is the only effective discipline.

There seems to be some evidence to support the belief that an occasional spanking, if the relationship between the child and parent is satisfactory, does no particular harm. But the question here is: Does a spanking do any real good? It is difficult to answer except to emphasize that there is always a better way to deal with children than through physical punishment.

DO USE THE FAMILY COUNCIL

An important institution in a democratic family should be the family council. Most parents find it difficult to sit down with their children as equal partners to discuss family problems and to arrive at solutions. But unless family council sessions are conducted regularly, the family will rarely function smoothly, because its members are inclined to think only of their own wishes, needs, and intentions.

It is difficult for a mother to be responsible for a well-knit, well-run family, and yet the concept of a "good" mother is that she alone is responsible. If she abdicates this manipulating position to any degree, she is regarded too often as a failure. The picture of a loving, giving, responsible mother is held up by professional and lay people alike. Yet without this overwhelming feeling of responsibility and the inevitable fear of neglecting a duty, the mother could enjoy her role in life and the children could enjoy more independence and responsibility.

The family council should *not* be conducted primarily for the purpose of assigning household chores; it is a forum where every family member has the opportunity to present his view with regard to any of the functions of the household, or, for that matter, anything regarding his relationship with other members of the family. Discussions should be free and open; every member of the family should be entitled to his say and his vote. The meetings should be held at regular intervals, and the chairman should rotate so the children do not feel that meetings are always controlled by the parents.

When parents are first confronted with the prospect of such a meeting, they become quite apprehensive about the possible consequences, particularly if they have more than two children. On the surface their fears pertain to mistaken judgments the children might make. These fears are groundless, though there is inevitably a testing period in the beginning when the children experiment with their newfound power. Parents who are not easily frightened will welcome the children's mistaken recommendations, and the children will be impressed with their own faulty decisions and will eventually exercise the better judgment of which they are capable.

The family council provides one of the most effective means of teaching children how to evaluate adequately the problems which come up in families.

There seems to be a law that only children have the right to be clever. It is our purpose to help parents to be a match for children, and the family council is one of the best opportunities. The following example concerns a mother with three teen-age girls, whom she manages to win over by treating them as equals in the family council situation.

> At an early family council meeting the three girls announced that now that they had the majority, they were going to set up their own rules about going out at night on dates. They were going to go out as often as they pleased, and would not be required to telephone and tell their mother where they were or when they would be home. The mother argued against this position but wisely refrained from being arbitrary about the matter, although she registered her vote as being against the proposal. Several days later she went to visit a friend, having told no one but her husband. She stayed there all night, did not telephone and did not arrive at home until about ten o'clock the next morning. The girls, quite agitated, demanded to know where she had been and why she had not told them where she was going. Her reply was very calm: "At the last family council meeting we voted to go out when we pleased and not notify anybody when or where we went. After all, if this rule applies to you, it applies to me as well." At the next family council meeting the girls were quite willing to set up more sensible rules of conduct with respect to dating.

The family council can be used to designate household duties, especially those that may not be apparent to the children. The duties of the father are to provide for the family's livelihood; the mother cooks and washes clothes; the children clean up their rooms and take care of their possessions. Other household chores should be mentioned at family councils, and children can be asked which ones they choose to undertake. If the atmosphere is one of give-and-take, someone will be found to do even the unpleasant jobs. Experience has indicated that job performance is much more likely to be facilitated by agreement than by arbitrary parental assignments. At subsequent councils performance can be analyzed and chores reassigned to meet the choice of everyone.

It is important for children to realize that responsibilities around the house belong not only to parents. If the child fails to live up to his responsibility, the parent should do so too. If the children do not wash the dishes, mother does not cook their next meal. If they are unwilling to hang up their clothes, then the clothes do not get washed and ironed. If this method is adhered to, the children soon realize that a well-functioning household demands cooperation from all the members; furthermore, their own welfare is enhanced by what they contribute as well as what they receive.

CHAPTER 6

THE USE OF LOGICAL CONSEQUENCES

Encouragement and logical consequences are two of the most important techniques parents can use to improve relationships with their children. More important, they supplant the outmoded traditions of reward and punishment that are proving to be less and less effective. Reward and punishment are products of an age when people believed in absolutes. Today, when distinctions between what is good and evil are increasingly difficult to define, the individual is being called upon to make decisions based on his own experience rather than on established rules. In order to help children develop such an experience so they can make complex decisions, parents must rely upon different methods to prepare them.

Although the idea of logical consequences comes from a concept suggested by Herbert Spencer more than a hundred years ago, its wisdom was ignored then. The principle, briefly expressed, states that *no person will willingly do what he believes is harmful to himself.* The reason we do so many things which ultimately harm us is that at a given moment we believe mistakenly that a particular course of action is the best, or at least the safest. One can see the illustration of the safety principle most clearly with the behavior of young children. If the child bumps his head on a table or puts his hand on a hot stove, his immediate response is to avoid that hazard next time. There is no need for further conditioning or reinforcing his response, as the behavioristic psychologists insist is essential.

The logical consequences premise is much the same as the safety principle. The child experiences the unpleasant result of his own actions, but the result is more or less arranged by the parent. There is another important difference: the result arranged by the parent can be distasteful or annoying to the child, but not harmful. Here is an illustration.

> Joseph, age 2, stepped in a mud puddle and got his shoes wet. He came into the house for dry clothes. When he asked to go out again, his shoes were not yet dry and therefore he was unable to go. In a matter-of-fact way he was told by his mother, "I am sorry, but your shoes are still wet."

Even a child of two is able to understand that if he gets his shoes wet he cannot play outside, particularly if the weather is damp or rainy. Furthermore, he comprehends without the usual lecture on the dangers of catching a cold and remonstrations to watch out for puddles, which is typical of most parents. The child would probably not have understood a lecture, but he *will* see the relationship between his act and the consequence. Even much older children can quickly see the connection between their own behavior and the result if it is properly presented.

> Two teen-age daughters chose to leave the dishes for their mother. She left them until the time for another meal. She prepared the meal in an untidy kitchen and announced the meal was ready. The girls found enough clean dishes to set the table. After the meal they took off and left the house and the dishes in a mess. The mother left the house also and did not return until after suppertime. Everybody was home amid the dirty mess with no meal and no mother. The girls reaped the consequences by washing the mess of dry, smelling dishes before the meal was prepared. They now say, "The sooner the dishes are washed, the better." This lesson is several years old but remains fresh in their minds.

This example also illustrates an important point in all relationships with children, particularly teen-agers: although you cannot force them to do what they choose not to do, neither can they force you to do anything that you do not want to do. When the children did not carry out their part of the bargain by washing the dishes, the mother indicated by her absence that she would not prepare a meal until there were clean dishes on which to serve it. Though adolescents expect and demand many services, they can be made to realize that cooperation is a two-way street. Services could be withheld when they do not cooperate, not on a tit-for-tat basis as retaliation but as a logical and understandable consequence of their behavior.

However, as most parents realize when they attempt to use logical consequences, the principle behind the concept is deceptively simple but the application is not. A way to understand logical consequences more clearly is to contrast logical consequences with punishment as it is currently practiced today.

DIFFERENCES BETWEEN LOGICAL OR
NATURAL CONSEQUENCES AND PUNISHMENT

Punishment is as old as human history. It probably dates from the time when man first began to establish communal societies for self-protection; accordingly, laws became necessary to protect individuals against others who might exploit them. Obviously, penalties were necessary in order to enforce these laws. However, with the development of authoritarianism, the motives behind punishment changed; instead of being a means to protect the individual against those who violated laws, punishment became a method by which those in power enforced their demands upon their subjects.

The concepts of right and wrong also became vehicles for this control. Those in command were superior and therefore right; those whom they ruled were inferior and wrong if they disagreed with the rulers. Punishment was the fate of those who disobeyed. This punishment was necessarily retaliatory rather than a corrective deterrent to potential offenders. Punishment was effective as long as society supported the power of the authorities, but with the development of democracy and the breaking down of the distinction between "superiors and inferiors," the effectiveness of punishment vanished.

Today most adults who punish do not see that punishment is still retaliatory rather than corrective. However, a child who is beaten sees the punishing authority as trying to impose his will by brute force. Because the child resents the action and refuses to accept the authority as sacrosanct, he tries to find ways of defeating it. As a result, whatever corrective effort the adult had in mind is wasted. Since punishment, like sin, is still so much a part of our tradition and upbringing, most of us believe that children cannot learn to function as mature adults in this society without it, and we continue to use the old autocratic methods without being fully aware why they no longer work.

It is interesting to note that in certain primitive cultures the concepts of reward and punishment are rarely utilized in rearing children. In her descriptions of a South Sea island tribe, the Arapesh, Margaret Mead [1] shows how parents employ what could be called a method of logical consequences. Children are not scolded; they are *helped* if they get into difficulties. Little children are taught not to suppress emotions, but to see that emotional expression harms no one but themselves. Little girls wear pretty grass skirts which would be ruined by the mud if they indulged in temper tantrums. They are taught also to carry small bags on their heads by "permitting" them, as a great favor, to carry their parents' possessions; to spill the contents would be a pity. As a result, the little girls appear to control their fits of rage and crying earlier than the boys.

In this tribe there is no distinction between the social status of children and of adults, so characteristic of "civilized" cultures. No age or sex is superior. Consequently, the terms grandfather, uncle, brother, and son are used interchangeably; the same person can be called by any one of these names, depending on how one feels about him at the moment. The Arapesh form a group with almost complete social equality. However, it is perhaps pertinent to note that in most areas of the South Seas, where the physical means of subsistence and existence have always been relatively easy to

[1] Margaret Mead, *From the South Seas.* New York, William Morrow, 1939.

secure, the extremes of social inequality appear to be less prevalent. Perhaps this is the reason why many of us envy the Polynesians with their relative lack of complexity, anxiety, and the inequities which beset our "civilized" cultures.

As we in America move away from authoritarianism to a more democratic way of life, we must unlearn centuries of habit and tradition, the roots of which are deep in every family structure. We are beginning to understand why reward and punishment are outdated remnants of the autocratic past, and why we need new methods to ensure equality for our children as well as ourselves.

1. Logical consequences express the reality of the social order, not of the person; punishment, the power of a personal authority.

> Joe, age 8, simply would not get himself dressed in time to get to school. Often he could not decide what to wear. Mother would scold him, nag him, often end up selecting his clothes for him and then driving him to school because his friends had already left. Threats and tears, nagging and spanking were all to no avail. Finally one day in utter exasperation she said to Joe, "I'm sick and tired of nagging you. It's up to you to decide what to do, but I am not going to drive you to school today." Now it was Joe's turn to put on a temper tantrum, with tears, and recriminations. And all to no avail. Joe walked to school by himself and was a half hour late. The next day Joe was dressed on time and waiting for his friends to come by and pick him up to walk to school.

What is the crucial element in the "social order" which prevailed after the mother had failed to convince Joe with her entreaties and threats? It is *time*. Most of us have to get up at a certain time, go to school or work at a certain time, and eat at a certain time; thus we are able to organize ourselves more efficiently in our life tasks. But since it is society which establishes the time school starts and not the mother, and since the mother decided to remove herself from the picture and let Joe experience the discomforts of being late to school and walking by himself, no further correcting was needed. Though Joe may not necessarily have used mother's scoldings and spankings as retaliation, the implications are there: "If you do not dress at a certain time I will spank you." What Joe did see, although he was not consciously aware of it, was that his tantrums got his mother involved, excited, and upset, and as long as she was involved he could see no result of his own act.

The social order presents the rules for living which all human beings must learn in order to function effectively. Many rules may be purely cultural, others have the universality which transcends specific societies. For instance, the use of the knife and fork in eating may vary from culture to culture, but the penalty for killing someone else unjustifiably is generally quite severe in all societies. It is also true that many rules of a society are not necessarily just or even helpful to individual welfare. But the point here is not to discuss the merits or demerits of certain rules, but to illustrate that they are established by the whole society and are not a whim of the parent or adult in immediate authority. As a result rules can be valuable allies to the parent in getting the child to see the relationship between his own act and the result. The child who has come home late for dinner is usually scolded and perhaps even spanked. But the proper logical consequence is for the mother to put the food on the table and he can eat it whenever he arrives, as long as the rest of the family is still eating. At the conclusion of the meal if the child has not arrived, the dishes are cleared and he gets no dinner that day. Another example of a logical consequence: a child who fails to clean up his room at the proper time must delay his favorite television program until he has completed his work. Thus the social order in any culture consists of a body of rules which operates on an impersonal level and must be learned in order for the child to function adequately.

2. The logical consequence is logically related to the misbehavior; punishment rarely is.

> There was difficulty with a 13-year-old daughter who would not hang up her clothes. She not only dropped them when she had pulled them off, but seemed to delight in wadding them up. She had been fairly good about her clothes when she was younger and the mother did not understand her change. After trying reasoning, threatening, and scolding, the mother finally told the girl to go ahead and throw them down, adding that she would not pick them up for her, or iron them as long as she threw them around. The daughter complained she did not have enough to wear, but the mother refused to do anything about it until the girl took care of what she had. She wore soiled and wrinkled clothes to school a few times before she began to be more careful. It was not long before the daughter picked up her clothes.

When the girl realized that she alone was responsible for having to wear wrinkled and dirty clothing to school, the misbehavior was quickly corrected. Such a procedure, of course, takes a while to achieve results and the parent must be patient.

Unfortunately, punishments like scolding or spanking are used in most situations and children come to regard them as arbitrary acts, even though the parents' motive is to correct. Children see little relationship between punishments and their own acts, and they resolve to get even or to find some way around the parental action so they can continue doing what they are doing.

Essentially, the child must *see* the relationship between his own behavior and the result, or the consequence, will not work.

3. *Logical consequences imply no element of moral judgment; punishment often does.*

> Mother caught her daughter in a bald-faced lie. "Donna, you know it is very wrong to lie. People who tell lies get to the point where they can't be honest and straightforward. Their souls become miserable and mean. Do you think that God and all his saints have any use for such people? God wants us to be honest and truthful. There is no place in heaven for wrong-doers. When you lie you are not good." [2]

This example is a misuse of religious principles which can discourage and often frighten a small child. Whenever a parent threatens a child with punishment by God, there may be one of two results. Because the child is unable to be good all the time, his fear of being punished by some mysterious authority for any insignificant wrongdoing may increase anxiety and insecurity to the degree that he may be afraid to risk doing anything. An older and more sophisticated child quickly discovers that no such punishment is forthcoming and learns to scoff at such a threat; at the same time he learns to see religion not as an inspiration in striving for the good life but as a weapon his parent uses to frighten him into submission. Though as a rule it is difficult to impose a consequence for lying, sometimes a deliberate lie told by the parent to the child—who later finds out the truth for himself—may be far more effective than scoldings or admonitions, and certainly less dangerous than appeals to religion or to moral judgments.

One of the few concepts about which most psychologists agree is that moral judgments should be avoided in dealing with children. Unfortunately, as the above example shows, the traditional doctrine in the autocratic past has been to use moral judgment as a means of maintaining the power of an authority figure to effect a correction of misbehavior. Because the need of children to gain recognition is often a much stronger motive than their desire to conform, they are all too often burdened with guilt feeling because they violate rules they believe to be right. Because they have been taught to equate worth with being good, they become convinced that they are "no good," since it is impossible not to violate rules at times. As a consequence they may turn more and more to a useless, destructive direction in life; at least they gain recognition from adults, if not favorable attention. The concepts on which logical consequences are based presuppose that the child is born neither good nor bad, nor does he develop arbitrarily in either

[2] Rudolf Dreikurs and Vicki Soltz, *Children: The Challenge.* New York, Duell, Sloan & Pearce, 1964, p. 291.

direction. His acts may be judged good or bad by society, but this does not alter his essential value as a human being. His misbehaviors have to be recognized as mistakes rather than sins, and it is the responsibility of the adult to point this out without labeling the child as good or bad.

Punishment carries the connotation of sin. A child interprets his punishment to mean he has no value, that his parent or teacher has no faith in him as a worthwhile person. Logical consequences avoid making any judgment of this sort: they distinguish between the deed and the doer. The child who experiences the unpleasant consequences of his act in all likelihood will view the act as something to be avoided in the future. Furthermore, the child is relieved of the feeling that he is subject to the whim of an authority over which he has no control. A logical or natural consequence gives him the choice of deciding for himself whether or not he wants to repeat a given act.

4. Logical consequences are concerned only with what will happen now; punishments, with the past.

> The judge read over the record and then looked sternly at the boy before him. "This is the third time you have been here. You have again been convicted of car stealing. Apparently you are not able to learn from your past mistakes. What do you have to say for yourself?" The boy looked wearily at the judge and shrugged his shoulders. "I don't know," he mumbled. The judge said, "I have no further recourse but to sentence you to six months in the state reformatory. Perhaps this will be a lesson to you in the future."

Such scenes are repeated over and over thousands of times not only in this country but all over the world. Unfortunately, there is little hope for correction when the old biblical notion of an eye for an eye and a tooth for a tooth is employed. Again we see the relationship between the concept of sin and the old autocratic order. To atone for one's crime one must do penance by serving time in prison or paying a fine or both. The fallacies of such punishment are painfully clear. Unfortunately, there are still no guidelines or facilities in our judicial and penal system which might provide a sentence that is geared more to the time necessary for rehabilitation and which might make a logical consequence of the sentence. In order to do this, the judge would have to consider many factors surrounding the crime's enactment, social, economic, and personality factors which make each offender different. It is much easier to rely on a rigid statute, the origins of which may be hundreds of years old.

With few exceptions, the more years a man serves in prison, the *less* chance he has of avoiding crime when he is released. Supposedly, when you have "paid" for your crime, your debt to society is fulfilled; you are free to commit the same crime again if you are willing to "pay" for it.

On the other hand, the consequences, natural and logical, to the disturbance of order are self-evident and come into play only when the individual disregards order. There is no element of sin or penance involved. As soon as a child learns that an unpleasant result will inevitably follow in a given antisocial act, he will usually think twice before repeating it. Thus it becomes order and reality itself—not the arbitrary power of the adult or of the adult society—which brings about the unpleasant consequences. The parent can stand by as a friend because the child does not feel personally defeated. Also the element of bribery (in the form of reward for good behavior and punishment for bad) can be avoided.

5. *The voice is friendly when consequences are invoked; there is danger in punishment, either open or concealed.*

> "Sam, you come right here this minute!" The father's tone is angry and insistent. "How many times have I told you *not* to use my tools without asking permission? Now you go to your room immediately and stay there until I say you can come out."

Whether the father realizes it or not, the chances of the boy getting into his tools again are much greater than they would have been had he used a friendlier tone of voice. The tone of voice is a reliable gauge for human relationships; it indicates open or underlying attitudes.

The successful application of consequences presupposes that the adult is a friendly bystander. His tone of voice should genuinely imply a regret that under the given circumstances he cannot do anything else except let the child face the consequences of what he has done. A harsh tone belies any assumption of friendliness; it indicates anger, unspoken demands, the willingness to retaliate. Friendliness has to be genuine. If the parents feel threatened or defeated, they are in no position to apply logical consequences because they are too personally involved.

The technique of using consequences and personal disengagement depend on each other; one cannot take place without the other. And the tone of voice is the most reliable indicator of the personal involvement of the adult. One cannot conceal one's real attitude; the voice is a true barometer.

In the above example the father could have said quietly to the boy, "It appears that you cannot go into the garage without using my tools, even without my permission, so, until you are ready to ask permission first, you will have to stay out of the garage." If such a statement does not prevent the boy from entering the garage, it is relatively simple to put a lock on the door. In any case, the father then leaves the choice open to the boy to decide when he is willing to abide by the rules.

CONDITIONS UNDER WHICH LOGICAL CONSEQUENCES MAY BE UTILIZED

1. *The Use of Choice.* Choice is inherent in the nature of every logical consequence. The adult should always give the child a choice if possible. The child should be asked to choose between behaving in the correct manner or continuing with his misbehavior: if he decides to continue it, then the consequence should immediately follow.

> During the course of a family counseling interview, the mother disclosed that one of the major problems she had was getting George, age 4, to eat his regular food. It appeared all he wanted to eat was bread and milk. When the mother put food in front of him, he would complain loudly and not eat the food until he had been brought some bread and milk. It was recommended to the mother that at the next meal George be given the choice of eating just bread and milk or the regular meal. Mother was also asked whether or not George liked other foods besides bread and milk. She admitted there were several. It was suggested that she cook some of these foods but permit George to eat only bread and milk if he chose this. Upon the mother's return a week later, it was revealed that after three days of eating nothing but bread and milk, George was happy to eat anything that was placed before him.

There are some examples of logical consequences where a verbal choice, as in the situation above, is not feasible or desirable. For example, the child who dawdles while dressing and is subsequently late to school should not be offered a verbal choice of taking his time or speeding up his dressing. In fact, the wise mother would refrain from mentioning to the child that if he did not hurry he would be late for school. Obviously, after being late once or twice the choice would be clear in the child's mind and no further suggestion would need to be made.

A frequent error made by adults is offering the child his choice of "punishments" *after* he has misbehaved. The child either selects the easiest punishment or refuses to accept any of the choices. The adult is thereupon forced into a position of providing an arbitrary punishment, which only increases the conflict between himself and the child.

2. *Understanding the Goal of the Child.* As was indicated in Chapter 2, an understanding of the psychological goal of the child is vital to the success of any corrective measure. Generally speaking, logical consequences are most effective when the goal is attention getting. When the goal is power or revenge, the child is so busily engaged in either asserting his superiority over the adult or in getting even with him that he often does not care what results his actions incur. The more unpleasant the responses of the adult, the better they fit into the child's scheme, into his desire to fight

or to get even. Children in extreme states of emotional disturbance, anger, or hostility rarely perceive consequences as the result of their acts but only as the punitive expression of a controlling or revengeful adult (which they frequently are). If one wishes to use consequences with an emotionally disturbed child, one must be sure the consequences are not imposed by an adult, but are inherent in the situation. Natural consequences that take place without active interference by adults can be effective with children who are involved in a power contest or who seek revenge.

3. *The Situation of Danger.* Critics of logical consequences always point out the specific examples where logical consequences obviously cannot be used. There are, of course, many such instances. A child cannot be permitted to run out in the street and be hit by a car to prove that automobiles are dangerous. There are many situations where simple prohibition, followed by removal of the child to a safer location, is the most effective answer. A skilled adult can, however, transform these situations into consequences through proper handling. A child who runs out into the street should be calmly and firmly placed in the backyard so he cannot get out, or in a room he is unable to leave; he should be told that when he is ready to play in the front yard without running into the street, he may return. After a period of time the adult should ask the child if he thinks he is ready to play in the yard; if the child says "yes," he should be allowed to play outside. If he attempts to run out in the street again, he should be immediately returned to the backyard or the house for a longer time. This episode rarely has to be repeated more than a few times in order for even a very young child to grasp the significance of his own actions and the consequences.

4. *When Consequences Fail.* Various types of consequences and their application will be discussed later in detail, utilizing case studies as examples.

If, however, a consequence is tried and is found to be ineffective, it is important to analyze step by step each action in the situation to find where the source of error might lie. Though often painful to the adult, writing down these steps can be an invaluable aid in objective analysis. Frequently the error will be found in the adult's behavior, such as arbitrary command, an "I told you so!" attitude at the outcome, a scolding or reprimand tainting the consequence. After such an analysis, the adult will understand better how to apply logical consequences.

It must be emphasized that despite the many applications suggested for the use of logical consequences, each attempt involves an element over which the adult has no control: How does the *child* view the situation? Success or failure depends as much on this factor as any other. In the beginning there may be more failures than successes, as examples in subsequent chapters will show. But time and experience in the application of logical consequences (with the resultant gain in understanding of children) will find successes outnumbering greatly the failures. Failures and mistakes will never be eliminated entirely, but we feel the concept of logical consequences is so uniquely adapted to the need of today's increasingly democratic culture that mistakes are far less likely to be psychologically damaging to the child than those in the name of punishment. For this reason an adult can use logical consequences with high hope and—most important—with a clear conscience.

TO REVIEW AND SUMMARIZE
THE CHAPTER ON LOGICAL CONSEQUENCES:

Logical Consequences	vs. *Punishment*
1. Express the reality of the social order, not the person.	Expresses the power of a personal authority.
2. Are intrinsically related to the misbehavior.	Does not include a logical, only an arbitrary, connection between misbehavior and consequences.
3. Involve no element of moral judgment.	Inevitably involves some moral judgment.
4. Are concerned only with what will happen now.	Deals with the past.

The user of logical consequences must understand that the technique is not applicable in all situations, that it is most successful in dealing with attention-getting misbehaviors. The adult must try to fathom the goal of the child before proceeding. Logical consequences should offer the child a clear and logical choice of behavior and results. The child must perceive that he has a choice and accept the relationship of his choice to what follows. The adult should try to be objective, but interested, in the situation and its outcome, and must always remember that he is involved in a learning process—not in a judicial proceeding. Instead of being angry, the adult should be understanding, sympathetic, "firm but fair"; if he is, the chances of the child learning the valuable insights which lead to the only workable method of discipline—self-discipline—will be greatly enhanced.

CHAPTER 7

CONFLICT SOLVING
THROUGH CONSEQUENCES

We have described the various aspects of applying consequences, so that anyone can design a great variety of responses to emerging conflict situations. A firm and definite knowledge of what should be done enables parents to respond properly without examining each situation, contemplating what to do, and then making the decision. As in the past, when everybody knew what to do in a conflict, the new methods of problem solving through logical consequences soon will be applied as automatically and naturally as reward and punishment.

Logical consequences permits an immediate response to interpersonal difficulties which arise within the family. Part of the basic technique of logical consequences is to solve problems through democratic transactions; this has been known to resolve conflicts instantly. Let us examine some of the basic principles.

PROBLEM SOLVING THROUGH
DEMOCRATIC TRANSACTIONS

Conflicts of interest, ideas, and desires are inevitable wherever people live together. In an autocratic past conflicts were resolved primarily through the use of reward and punishment, through pressure from without. Since punishment is no longer effective, we are groping for new yardsticks. It is the purpose of this book to provide them. Several principles are involved in the use of logical consequences. The four principles below should be regarded as the essential requirements for conflict solving in a democratic transaction.

1. All conflicts can be resolved only on the basis of mutual respect. This excludes fighting or giving in. Fighting violates respect for the opponent; giving in, respect for oneself. Logical consequences permit an alternative.

2. In any conflict situation one has to pinpoint the *real* issue. And the real issue is *never* the whole of the conflict; underneath each argument is the problem of personal involvement on the part of each participant, personality concerns like status and prestige, the desire to win, the fear of

losing, of being unfairly treated, of being deprived of one's rights. By not recognizing the importance of personal involvement, people turn mere disagreement into unsolvable conflicts.

Parents and teachers must see the total picture of their conflicts with children. Conflict is always based on the child's mistaken goals of attention, power, revenge, and withdrawal. These four goals are the basic issue between parents and younger children. The same holds true for the conflicts between adults; regardless of what the bone of contention may be, it always is a question of status, esteem, deprivation, and unfairness.

3. Conflicts can be resolved only by agreement. Instead of agreeing to fight, to overpower, or to abuse, the participants in the conflict must agree to work out an amicable solution. Few people realize that any relationship, whether good *or* bad, is based on agreement, on full cooperation and communication. That is to say, one cannot fight without communicating such intention to one's opponent and winning his full cooperation to fight it out.

Realizing that every transaction between two people is based on agreement, one does not need to feel frustrated or uncertain about the need to reach a better form of agreement. The existing consent cannot be maintained if one party refuses to continue his role in the agreed-to fight. The agreement can be changed if one or both parties of the conflict begins to think in terms of what *he* could do, instead of pointing out what his opponent should do in order to resolve the conflict.

We have an excellent demonstration of this principle in a dialogue. If one reads only the lines of one actor, omitting those of the second, then the words make no sense. Unfortunately, this is what most people do in a conflict: they hear only the lines the opponent speaks, and they make no sense. One frequently expresses astonishment about how the other person could be so unreasonable, mean, selfish, or what other epithet one chooses to describe the behavior of one's opponent. It makes no sense until one begins to hear one's own lines. But few people are willing to be so objective about themselves.

Reaching agreement is relatively simple if one is prepared to change one's own role and behavior. The effects of logical consequences are a powerful demonstration of one's own ability to resolve conflict, because the parent is eliminated from the position of an antagonist and sparring partner.

4. Conflicts can be resolved only through *participation* in decision making, through *shared* responsibility. Cooperation has to be won instead of demanded; that is, the opponents have to decide in favor of peace instead of war. Logical consequences permit everyone, but especially the child, to decide how to respond to the new situation.

Our task is not primarily to design various forms of consequences; innumerable answers to conflict situations are possible and will be found by parents who have learned to operate on the basis of the above four principles of conflict solving. What is needed now is a clear understanding of the way consequences are applied. The basic principles of conflict solving can be used as a reliable yardstick to indicate proper and improper uses of consequences.

CONFLICT SITUATIONS

Every day in the average American family conflicts between parents and children arise. Some are almost universal, others are unique. Behind all conflicts, however, lie the same basic issues: the war between the generations, the mistaken goals of the child, the parent's inclination to be deceived by the provocation because the parent has not learned to deal with the basic issue or the incident. Certain domestic situations lend themselves easily to the creation of conflicts: getting children out of bed in the morning; getting them ready for school; dressing them properly; getting them to eat and to develop proper eating habits; stopping them from fighting with their brothers and sisters; getting them to keep their room tidy, to take on responsibility for household chores, to do their homework; guiding their behavior in public places like the supermarket and restaurants; visiting friends at home or away; coming home on time and getting to bed at a reasonable hour. With older children the main problems are when to come home, especially with girls, and how and when to use the family car, a problem with boys.

The variety of situations that can lead to conflict is unlimited. There is a general principle, however. When the relationship between parents and children is tenuous, the conflict the child creates depends usually on the vulnerable point of the parent. As soon as the child realizes the parent's sensitivity to certain forms of conduct, the child often practices the conduct which the parent cannot tolerate.

> Mary, age 6, behaved in a most unusual and alarming fashion. She crawled on the floor with her hands bent as if they were paws. She did not speak or obey; instead, she barked. Her peculiar behavior led to the suspicion that she was mentally sick. What the counselor did not realize was that Mary's mother could not stand dogs. When Mary wanted a dog, her mother bought her one, but she did not permit the dog to enter the house. So Mary played "dog" instead.[1]

Mary's behavior appears irrational as long as one does not see the well-

---

[1] Some of the examples in this chapter are taken from our previous publications; but here they are discussed in a different way, since we are concerned primarily with the parents' immediate reactions through logical consequences.

designed performance of the child to defeat her mother. It is usually the same situation in all families: the child reacts to the parent's particular interest and determination. For example, if parents are particularly interested in the child's eating, the child may be willing to go hungry and even, in extreme cases, to starve himself to death.

Not every child in the same family will zero in on the same parental weakness; some will refuse to eat and others will eat too much. Some will not get up in the morning, and others will decide to wake up early and disturb the family. Some children use passive means, while others rebel actively. Even the experts do not realize that fears and jealousies are directed against parents; they do not indicate the child's insecurity, but his attempt to impress the parents. Children develop fears when the parents are concerned with the child's jealousy and criticize him for it. The reaction of a confused parent reinforces the child's intention and misconduct.

Not all conflict situations lend themselves to the application of logical consequences. There are particularly those entailing danger: it would be preposterous to let a child be seriously hurt, although some controlled experiences of unpleasant and even painful consequences are possible. However, in every situation the parents can learn to extricate themselves, refusing to be drawn into warfare. Nobody has to fight with a child unless he decides to do so, and when he does, he violates the first and most important principle in the solution of conflicts.

GETTING UP IN THE MORNING

In many families the fight starts in the morning when the parents cannot persuade the child to get up. He has to be reminded, coaxed, and often threatened. Such procedure violates all four basic principles in conflict solving. The parents fight with the child and then give in; little do they know that they are giving in to the child's demands when they keep reminding him to get up. The parents cannot recognize their concession if they do not pinpoint the basic issue. They may believe that the reason for the conflict is the child's "inability" to get up, perhaps because he did not go to bed on time. But is that the real reason? Definitely not. The child wants to keep mother's service and attention; he demonstrates his power by not getting up when she wants him to, but only when he is good and ready. This is the issue.

Now let us consider the agreement between the child and the parents. The child is saying that he expects the parents to continue their efforts, and they agree to do so in a contest of win or lose. And the spoils of this conflict are equally divided: the child wins first, by not getting up, and then the parents get their glory by finally getting him out of bed. There is a ritual to the procedure, with slight variations occurring in each family;

every one of the participants knows in advance what will happen and is willing to cooperate with the other in the game. There is little chance for mutual responsibility, because the parents take on the responsibility and leave none to the child.

The solution to the conflict is simple if one accepts the basic principles of conflict solving and acts accordingly. To avoid fighting and giving in the parents must remove themselves from the conflict situation and recognize the basic issues. If they refuse to continue their role, it will be up to the child to decide whether he wants to get up or else be late for school. Obviously, tardiness at school is the natural consequence which would take place as soon as the parents remove themselves from the battlefield.

Many people ask: What difference does it make whether the child gets up by himself or is prodded several times by his parents? The whole relationship is altered between the child and his parents when they no longer are willing to give service or fight. The child has an opportunity to learn how to take care of himself, how to take on responsibility. In many cases this is the first step of a new and better relationship.

When the parents are burdened by their sense of responsibility and feel obliged to see to it that the child meets his obligations, they cannot stay out of the conflict, even if they try. And as long as they are available, the child will put the pressure on them. He knows very well how to do that. Even if the parents give the child an alarm clock and tell him that from now on he has to take care of himself, they will not succeed as long as they are concerned and worried and, at the last minute, step in. Under these circumstances the alarm clock is useless; the child simply turns it off and continues to sleep. Only when he is sure that the parents are no longer involved and will not come to his rescue will he want to take on responsibility. After all, he does not want to arrive late at school. However, if his teacher misunderstands the situation and tries to make the *parents* responsible for his being late for school, she plays into his hands and forces the parents into the continuation of their service.

The effect of a proper approach can be easily undone if a parent keeps himself involved, as in the following example.

Dick, age 12, could not get up on time. He usually did his homework late in the evening, and therefore was tired in the morning. His mother "understood" and was willing to awaken him three to five times. She succeeded in her efforts as little as she did the evening before when she wanted him to do his homework earlier. Dick was convinced that this was the reason for his difficulty, although he got up by himself on a morning when he had to leave early for a trip. When he was confronted with the purpose of his "inability" to wake up, he responded with a recognition reflex. It was not as easy to convince mother of the real reason for his difficulty, which he recognized immediately when he was confronted with it. It was explained to her that despite his "insight," he would not be willing to give up his pressure on her unless she stopped being concerned with his being on time and let him experience the consequences of his being late.

When Dick's mother found out that she could leave to Dick the responsibility of getting up, she bought him an alarm clock and told him to set it and get up by himself. Next morning she heard the alarm go off and then stop ringing. She listened and waited, but nothing happened. After a short while she went upstairs and found him asleep. She awakened him and told him to hurry up.

The mother started on the right track but did not follow through. Just at the moment when her child could have gotten the message, she stepped in. Unfortunately, this is a very frequent procedure. Just when children can learn from the consequences of their behavior, the parents try to protect them from it. Only when children fully realize they can no longer rely on parental protection are they willing to accept responsibility.

BEING LATE FOR SCHOOL

Getting up in the morning is usually only part of a general procedure during which the child needs prodding, coaxing, helping, and threatening in order to be ready on time. There are problems of dressing, of what to wear, of dawdling, of arriving late for breakfast, of eating the breakfast. Here is a description of one mother's conflict.

> Fred was particularly slow to "perk up" in the morning and took far more time than needed to prepare for school. He was expected to make his bed and gather his own books and clothing before leaving and he had trouble meeting these requirements. Mother and father decided how much time was needed before school for fulfilling his duties, then they set the alarm clock to allow enough time. He was to make his bed, and so forth, even if late for school; he should require no reminders.

> But what happened? Only with extreme restraint could mother refrain from reminding, nagging, calling out the correct time. As a result she had made a power struggle out of natural consequences. If she could be consistent in her silence, Fred could solve his own problem easily, because he did not wish to be late for school.

The solution which Fred's mother attempted was not a solution at all. It was a power struggle from the beginning, and that is why she could not extricate herself. The best logical consequence can be ruined by the parent's attitude. Fred's mother, by forcing him to be late as pressure and almost as punishment, prolonged and strengthened the struggle with her child.

Training children to be orderly, to pick up books, clothes, and toys, and to make beds requires special considerations. Mornings are not suitable for conflict solving; in fact, conflicts should be avoided in the morning if possible. The fight over being ready on time can take many turns and exhibit varying degrees of intensity.

> Sally, age 10, had difficulty getting up in the morning. On a particular morning her mother tried for the third time to get her up, which she finally did. But then mother had to hurry her up with the threat not to drive her to school if she was late. Finally Sally came to breakfast and read a comic book while eating. Mother was furious. "Put that book down and hurry up eating, it's late!" At that moment the phone rang and mother became involved in a long conversation with a friend. Suddenly Sally got anxious and asked mother to drive her to school. At that point mother declined. Mother remained firm, but Sally reminded her that she hadn't been tardy the whole year and mother should take her only once more. "You wouldn't want me to spoil my record, would you?" So mother yielded, told her friend she would call her back, and then drove Sally to school.

This is an approach used by children that seldom fails: an appeal to the parents' pride. Sally's mother very nearly got so involved with a friend that her child might have experienced the logical consequence of her slowness; but the situation backfired, depriving the child of an important experience.

The example below expresses what happens frequently when the parents weaken or fight, instead of being totally passive but benevolent bystanders.

> Linda, age 12, was the last child out of the house at least two mornings a week. Her mother always made certain that she was awake, but not necessarily out of bed. One week the inevitable happened: Linda appeared about nine thirty and had to deal with the situation strictly on her own when she walked in late to school.

In a sense the example shows a natural consequence, but it occurred accidentally and was not planned by anyone. Therefore, despite experiencing the consequences of her behavior, Linda probably did not learn too much from it. Mother still feels obliged to make sure that Linda is at least awake at the proper time, so the whole atmosphere of service continues. One can assume why Linda's mother acts this way. She may believe that Linda, in order to decide that she has to get up, has to be awake. This implies that when Linda is not awake, she cannot take on responsibility, a mistaken assumption that is the cause of the girl's not being ready until nine thirty. It is difficult for parents to believe that the child can decide when it is time to get up, even if he is asleep, and particularly if he has an alarm clock. Training children to assume responsibility requires more faith in their ability to do so from their parents.

Lunchtime was a daily hassle for mother, who was having trouble getting Carol, age 6, off on time for afternoon kindergarten. Then she heard about the system of applying logical consequences. After a few days of contemplation, she decided to show Carol where the hands of the clock would be when it was time for her to leave for school, and then sat down to lunch with her. Carol dawdled. When mother finished eating, she left the table and sat in another room with a book. Carol finally left for school a half hour late. Mother continued with the procedure the next day. On the third day she wrote a note to the teacher asking for her cooperation. Carol was forty-five minutes late that day. When she came home, she was crying because the teacher had scolded her. "I am sorry you were late, dear. Perhaps you can manage better tomorrow," mother said. From that day on, Carol watched the clock like a hawk, and her mother ceased being concerned with getting her off on time.

When Carol's mother pretended to be no longer concerned about her daughter going late to school, Carol began testing her by going to school later each day; she realized, no doubt, that her mother was sitting on pins and needles. Only when the mother, in her defeat, called on the teacher to be her ally did the girl respond. She probably was not aware of mother's interference; otherwise, she might have continued her tardiness as an act of defiance toward her mother. Mother's "sympathetic" encouragement, which was somewhat dubious, saved the day, and Carol became willing to conform. However, there is an important lesson here: one should not pretend to be uninvolved if one continues to be involved. Children have an amazing ability to discern whether parents mean what they say. Most failures to succeed with logical consequences are due to pretenses which children recognize. Instead of being stimulated to proper behavior, the child feels almost honor bound to call the parent's bluff.

The following approach seems to have succeeded; but did it? The report is a history of a power struggle.

Helen, age 15, had her parents in a state of frustration every morning when she ran to catch the 7:20 A.M. bus to high school. Her alarm rang at 6:00 and she got up promptly. She was meticulous, and slow, about the application of makeup, about grooming her hair. Her parents would frequently warn her that she had only three minutes to catch the bus. She would reply calmly that she saw no reason to get there ten minutes early and wait in the cold. Usually she caught the bus at the last possible second, but on several occasions she missed it, and her father or mother drove her. They both resented this extra chore when there was no time for it, and told her so. However, things did not change until one cold morning when she missed the bus and her father told her, "Start walking, Helen. If you walk fast enough, you will even be on time." Helen did not miss the bus for the next three weeks.

Helen decided what she wanted to do with no regard for what her parents expected of her. The parents were thoroughly defeated by Helen —except for the effective last step they took—and one can well imagine that the elimination of one conflict area did not prevent their defeat in others. When the parents warned Helen, they were in reality servicing her. Helen's success was even more obvious when she forced her parents to drive her to school against her will. Finally, when the father refused to drive her to school, which he could have done quietly and much more effectively, he delivered the ultimatum as an autocratic demand, which is much like punishment. One can well assume the high price the parents thereafter paid for their "victory."

One has to utilize logical consequences in a democratic spirit. There is little evidence of mutual respect found in the above example. The parents tried to overpower Helen and in turn were defeated. What was the real issue of the conflict? Helen expressed it clearly: she wanted to have her own way, to concentrate on her personal appearance rather than the needs of the situation. Because her parents took on the responsibility, enabling her to get by, Helen never learned to respect them.

> Sue, age 7, was to catch the school bus at 7:20 A.M. She had been dawdling every morning and mother fell into her trap by reminding and pushing. When mother became aware of this, she was determined to let Sue be responsible for her own business. The next morning she dawdled as usual. Mother refrained from glancing at the clock, even surreptitiously. Sue left late. Shortly she returned with a sheepish look, half tears, half smile. "The bus left; I saw it turn just as I got to the corner." Mother replied that she was sorry Sue didn't make it. Sue went to her room to change to playclothes and then came out to involve mother in her affairs. Mother said, "Honey, I have my day's work to do just the same as if you were in school." Sue returned to her room to amuse herself. Later she came out again. "Mother, I am going out to ride my bike." "I am sorry, Sue, you can't ride your bike during school hours." "Oh," she responded, taken aback with this new thought. She continued to remain in her room, playing for the rest of the day with the exception of the lunch break during which she and mother enjoyed their conversation. Sue was not late for the bus for the next several months.

Again the mother's response in the situation appears very effective. She let Sue experience unpleasant consequences by not playing with her or letting her ride her bike, but she did allow Sue to amuse herself in her own room. The undisturbed play plus a pleasant conversation during lunch could be compensation in Sue's mind for missing the bus.

Generally, there is only one accepted reason for not being in school: to be ill. A child who does not go to school for whatever reason should be treated like a sick child. He should be kept in bed, fed a liquid diet, and refused the pleasure of radio and TV. This makes staying home undesirable. Of course any application of logical consequences like the above is impossible with a child in a power conflict. Had Sue been in a power struggle with her mother, the latter could not have resisted spending time with her.

As a rule one should deal with one issue at a time. Much depends on whether the child likes to go to school. If the child enjoys school, missing it is consequence enough. Then it is most important that mother does not get involved with the child. If the school is nearby, the child who misses the bus should walk and be late and then experience the consequences when he arrives at school. However, if the child enjoys being home instead of in school, more careful plans are needed to counteract the desire to stay home. Logical consequences do not resolve deeper conflicts and disturbances which may require planned procedures beyond the immediate moment.[2]

The situation below is a good example of what a logical consequence should *not* be.

> Although she arose at 6:00 A.M. daily, arranging her hair required so much time that Rose missed the 7:40 bus on an average of twice a week. When she would find that her classmates were no longer standing on the bus corner, Rose would run home again and her mother would back the car out of the garage for a hectic clock-racing trip to junior high school.

> Several "never-again-will-I-do-this" warnings were not effective. One day, as Rose dashed out of the house, probably too late to catch the bus, her mother told her not to return home, expecting a ride to school. When she realized that she had missed the bus again, Rose began walking in the direction of the school. Only a block away she was rescued by a friend who was being driven to school by her mother. The following week Rose twice had the same good fortune. Thus the logical consequence was being defeated by circumstances.

> The mother reasoned that Rose's good luck would run out. If not, she might seek the cooperation of several neighborhood mothers who drive their children to school. She could ask them either to overlook Rose as she hikes to school, or ask them to shift their routes just enough to avoid passing her.

Mother misses the point altogether. She wants Rose to be punished for her negligence and is willing to connive with others to bring that about. The logical consequence is not defeated "by circumstances," as mother

---

[2] See Rudolf Dreikurs and Vicki Soltz, *Children: The Challenge.* New York, Duell, Sloan & Pearce, 1964.

believes, but by her own misapplication. She clearly considers logical consequences as a gimmick to force the girl into appropriate action.

So far we have found that in regard to getting up and getting ready, all that is needed to let the child experience the consequence of being late instead of only going through the motion, the natural consequences of the situation come into play. Rose's mother did not intend to stay uninvolved. When she told the girl "not to return," she invited a power struggle in which the girl succeeded in outsmarting her. If she had removed herself from the situation instead of threatening to do so, Rose sooner or later would have found it preferable to be on time rather than to take the long way to school.

Very frequently the parents disagree about their responses to the child's provocation. Here is a typical dialogue between parents.

"Where is Penny?" daddy asked, as he sat down to breakfast.

"I thought she ought to sleep late this morning, dear."

"How come?"

"Well, she was up late last night. She wanted to see you before she went to bed."

"But I told you I would be very late."

"I know, but she doesn't understand that. So I let her stay up until she fell asleep."

"What about school today?"

"Oh, it won't matter. It's only kindergarten. I'll write a note that she wasn't well this morning."

"I don't know, Meg. It seems to me that Penny ought to follow some sort of rule."

"Oh, there is plenty of time for her to learn about rules. She is so little!"

The first prerequisite for the successful execution of logical consequences is to avoid fighting or giving in. Although the parents in the above example are not fighting—indeed, they seem to be having a friendly discussion—nevertheless, the question is: Who wins out, the father or the mother? Father has to let mother experience the consequences of their conflict with each other. He could discuss the problem with mother, but he would have to make sure that the mother is willing to listen; otherwise he has no right to impose his ideas on her. There is little he can say at the moment, except to admit that his ideas of training their daughter seem to be different from hers. Hopefully, later the father can exert his beneficial influence on the girl, who is being spoiled by the mother, by not giving in to her demands. He can let her experience the pressure of reality. Unfortunately, most parents want to have the other parent conform to *their* ideas before they even consider proper discipline of the child. Each one tries to make up for what he considers the deficiency of the other parent. When one parent seems too strict, the other tends to become permissive, and vice versa. There is no room left for the child to learn anything.

Here is an example of such a conflict between parents, in which one tried to dominate and the other submitted.

> Two boys, age 15 and 16, worked during the summer for their father. He left early in the morning and demanded that the two boys be in the shop by 9:00 A.M. Because of the distance, mother had to drive them. But the boys did not get up on time. Mother coaxed and pushed because father punished them when they were late by deducting from their pay. He not only demanded that mother get the boys to work on time but also that she tell him how late the boys were in order to figure the deduction. The mother sided with the boys against the father, thereby stimulating them to provoke father so that mother would feel sorry for them when father punished them.
>
> Being in the middle, she was blamed by both parties, by the father because she did not always tell him when the boys were late, by the boys because she sometimes did.

The principle of letting a logical consequence take place by extricating oneself from the conflict applies here. Mother did not need to wake the boys up or tell father when they were late; it was their business, not hers. It did not take her long to realize how she made herself a doormat for both parties; and as soon as she quit serving them, they came to an agreement. There was no need for the boys to provoke father when mother no longer felt sorry for them.

This brings us to another frequent problem which parents feel unable to solve. How can parents refrain from nagging, coaxing, and helping a child who is late in the morning when the parents themselves have to leave on time for work?

> Teddy, age 4, had achieved total independence in dressing himself until his sister was born. He knew well that his parents had to leave home at a specific time because they had to be at work on time. But he still managed to turn every morning into a struggle by dawdling and fussing until mother was forced by lack of time to dress him at the last moment. Mother arranged the morning so that he and she could share a leisurely breakfast without interruptions from the baby; but he still wasted time, so mother had to dress him completely. Any effort to praise Teddy would have been futile since he knew he could dress himself without help. After a few unusually chaotic mornings, mother simply put his clothes on his bed, handed him his coat, and told him he could dress in the car, because it was time to go and mother couldn't wait. This procedure required a few repetitions until he became ready to be dressed and on time without repeated warnings.

There are many ways to escape the well-designed efforts of a child to stymie parents who have to leave home on time. A neighbor, a baby-sitter, or a relative can step in and see to it that the child gets to school whenever he is ready. This person needs to be informed of the desired approach, that is, not to fall for the child's demands but to stand firm. The main point is the child's recognition that he can no longer put his parents into his service.

Here is an example of the effects which can be achieved by an outsider, even if the parents find it difficult to use the proper approach.

> It was literally a Herculean effort for 7-year-old Jean's mother to get her off to school on time. She always had a delaying tactic. One morning her dress was not properly ironed. On another occasion it was not really the one she wanted to wear. Often the right garments were never around, and the indulgent mother had to find them before the child would dress. Somehow Jean always got to school on time; but mother felt she was becoming a nervous wreck, simply getting her to the point where she was ready to go to school. Shortly thereafter, mother became ill and had to go to the hospital for an immediate operation. Since father had to leave for work before Jean left for school, a neighbor was asked to look after Jean and see that she was taken care of before and after school. Toward the end of her hospitalization, mother asked the neighbor how she had fared in getting Jean to school. "That was no problem," the woman replied. "When I saw what a fuss she was making, I just said, 'Well, you can go to school whenever you please.' The first two mornings she was late; and after that there were no more problems." Taking the cue from her neighbor, mother repeated this statement when she returned home, and found to her surprise that Jean was dressed and ready for school without any difficulty.

GETTING DRESSED

Procrastination in dressing is a reason for getting to school late, as we saw in several examples. Good dressing habits are one of the first responsibilities a child has to assume, and the first which confronts him as he gets up in the morning. Often it is a source of conflict and turmoil; the parent, especially the mother, is torn between her sense of responsibility and her anger about the child's inability or unwillingness to assume his. In the ensuing struggle the child usually wins by putting mother in his service. Presently we underestimate considerably the ability of the very young child; often it becomes obvious in an indirect way.

> Paul, age 2, could not put on his shirt. He always put it on with the front in the back. It never occurred to mother that he must know how the shirt should be put on in order to avoid putting it on properly.

Guy, age 4, consistently put his shoes on the wrong feet. This annoyed mother considerably. "For heaven's sake, Guy, when will you learn to put your shoes on right? Come here." Then the mother sat him down to change his shoes.

In both cases the mother does not realize the reason for her child's "ineptness." Once she is aware and really convinced of the fact that it is not a question of inability, but of unwillingness in order to get her service or defeat her, the proper response is obvious. The child does not like to be improperly dressed, although he may pretend that he does not care; he wants to continue to play his game. And as long as mother is more interested in the child's dressing properly than he is, he will take advantage of her.

There are two ways a mother can respond without fighting or giving in. In the morning she can let the child dress himself as he sees fit. If the dressing is done incorrectly, he will find out by his physical discomfort and the reaction of others. Then in the afternoon, after school, the mother can give the child dressing lessons, until he has learned to dress himself properly. This usually does not take long, since the child is not interested in using up his playtime after school to learn how to dress. It is amazing how quickly children learn when parents leave them to their own resources.

The striking part of the following example is how long it takes most mothers to realize how a problem can be solved.

Although Karen was 4 years old, she seemed to need quite a bit of help in getting dressed. She particularly disliked putting on her sox, which appeared to require too much effort on her part. One day mother decided to step out. Mother told Karen that she could put on her sox if she wanted, and mother then left the room. That was the last time there was any trouble. When Karen realized that mother was no longer going to help her, she put on her sox by herself.

The dressing problem has many variations.

Ralph, age 8, was spending about fifteen minutes each morning arguing over what he should wear to school: whether or not he needed a raincoat, sweater, or boots. Whatever mother said he needed, he would deny.

Mother decided one cold rainy morning not to say anything at all. Ralph put on his slicker over a short-sleeved shirt, certainly not enough warmth for such a cold day. Ralph left in the unheated car with his father for school, shivering all the way. He turned to his father and said in a very perturbed voice, "Mother doesn't care about what I wear to school, and I am just freezing."

The next morning Ralph checked the outdoor thermometer and morning weather report and dressed appropriately for school.

The above example has interesting implications. There is a tendency for spoiled children to blame parents for their own discomfort, like the boy who said, "I froze my hands because father didn't put my gloves on—now he will be sorry." This is a kind of reverse logical consequence, but in fact Ralph's remark about his mother's not caring has some justification. It was an act of hostility for the mother to choose an unusually cold day to teach Ralph a lesson. Logical consequences should not imply such punishment. There can be no doubt that the child learned his lesson, but there can also be no doubt about the child's future attitude toward his mother. Logical consequences should take the parent off the hook. The mother in this example put herself squarely on it.

The question of what clothes to wear lends itself wonderfully to arguments and fights.

> The mother of an 8-year-old girl was trying to get her daughter to realize that certain clothes were for certain occasions, that is, "good clothes" were to be worn to church and parties, school clothes to school and on ordinary occasions, and playclothes for afterschool activities, picnics, and so forth.
>
> Talking it over, nagging and scolding, did not work; so mother decided to let nature take its course. The girl continued to wear her good clothes to school and for play. One Saturday she asked her mother to wash a good dress so it could be worn to a birthday party that afternoon. The mother refused, saying she had many other things which had to be done.
> "Aha," thought mother. "She'll learn now to keep party clothes for parties." It did not work, however. The girl went to the party in her playclothes, had a wonderful time and was not at all self-conscious. Only the mother was embarrassed.

The logical consequence failed in this case because the mother used it as a gimmick, hoping to embarrass the child into wearing proper clothes at proper times. The girl was fully aware, as children usually are, of mother's intent, and she proceeded to punish mother by being improperly dressed. Mother was right in stopping her nagging and scolding, but instead of being uninvolved, she was waiting for the crucial moment when the child would recognize her poor judgment. It is evident that the girl's notion about what to wear was dictated by her rebellion against mother and her standards. Mother's reaction in the given situation clearly indicates the continuation of antagonism and fight. In such an atmosphere logical consequences immediately degenerate into acts of hostility.

Rick, age 5, was a holy terror, a tyrant. Whenever mother did not do what he wanted, he punished her, either by humiliating her or hitting his little brother. Getting him out of bed was a major undertaking, except of course on Sundays and holidays, when he not only got up by himself but rather early. His idea of proper clothes was very simple: he liked to wear his new and best clothes to kindergarten. If mother let him wear them, he dressed himself; if not, he refused to dress and mother had to dress him—which she did, in order to get him to kindergarten on time. Actually she could easily motivate Rick to get dressed on time, because he liked kindergarten very much, and certainly would not have wanted to miss it.

In some instances one can use the child's desire for breakfast to get him dressed. In this case Rick did not want to eat, either, and still had to be spoon-fed by his indulgent grandmother. The mother responded well to an explanation of her difficulties and of the procedures which she could use effectively. It turned out that her withdrawal from any conflict in the morning changed the whole relationship between herself and the boy. The extrication of herself from his tyranny in the morning was the first step in depriving him of the power which he wielded over her.

In many cases the termination of arguing and fighting in the morning is the initial step to general improvement. Instead of trying to assert her own power, the mother let Rick experience the power and pressure of reality, which even a power-drunk child can learn to respect.

Frank, age 10, was constantly misplacing his boots. The other members of the family had to join in the search, because if they waited for Frank to find them, they would all be late for school. It was finally agreed upon by everyone that Frank would have to keep track of his boots and find them himself. Dad would leave the house for school, and if Frank didn't have his boots, he could look for them until he found them, and mother would then drive him to school. The first time he couldn't find his boots and realized that dad and the other children were leaving without him, he cried and carried on. When he realized that crying was not getting him attention or his boots, he decided to find them. He was late for school, but after that he did not mislay his boots.

Although the application of the consequences induced the boy to be more careful with his boots, one wonders what other means to keep the family busy he may have continued to use. One gets the impression that only one particular form of behavior was altered, because the boy's initial response to not getting service was to cry. A child who uses his "water-power" in such a way usually succeeds in making others feel sorry for him. Therefore mother will have to be careful to stay apart from his problems and apply the consequences to other episodes like the lost boots.

Here is how another mother dealt with a boy who had boots trouble.

Sam, age 6, refused to wear boots to school when it was raining. One day it was, which led to the usual fuss. Mother said that he could wear boots or stay home, and further explained to him that if he remained home from school, it meant that he was sick and had to go to bed and stay there until well. Sam decided to stay home. He put on his pajamas and got into bed. Friends came after school to play and were told that Sam was sick and unable to play. The next morning and thereafter he wore boots when it was raining.

Many may argue that the mother dictated to Sam what to do. Actually she gave him a choice. And Sam no doubt understood that one has to wear boots when it is raining, as well as the fact that one has to be sick in order to not be in school. If the child was not literally sick, he must assume the role to meet the school regulations. Sam's mother was neither fighting with Sam nor giving in. This is the function of logical consequences.

It is interesting to note in the situation below that the parents sincerely tried to apply logical consequences. But a power conflict was evident at every turn of events; every new consequence resulted in a new act of defiance from the girl. Here is the report of the harassed mother.

Beth had sprouted out of her clothes, so new dresses had been bought for school. She wore one once and came home filthy, with grease stains and playground dirt. "I can wear this again before it is washed, can't I, Mother?" The mother got the impression Beth really wanted her to see how dirty she was. The subject of getting so dirty had been carefully explored at a family council meeting, and Beth had agreed that she perhaps engaged in robust play more than the situation warranted. She had agreed that she would be more careful. But now she stood in a mood of defiance. "Honey, if you don't care how you look, neither do I. However, I see no reason to have several dresses get dirty. You may wear this one." The mother removed all her dresses from the closet. Beth burst into tears. "I can take care of my clothes, really I can." At this point daddy interfered. "We will discuss it at the next council meeting." Beth brought it up immediately after a meeting was called to order several days later. "Can we discuss my clothes?" Mother said, "What about them?" "I want my dresses back. How can I show you I can take care of them if I don't have any?" Mother answered, "You have a point. Do you want to try again?" Beth said, "Yes. I don't have to get so dirty." The clothes were returned. However, during the four days before the dresses were returned, Beth failed to wash her hands before setting the table. The mother didn't observe it the first night until she was almost finished with dinner. Daddy saw it at the same time. "If you wish to have dirty hands, you may not be at the table with us." Beth left and her plate was removed. She returned but when she saw this she solemnly left again without a word. The following day she entered the kitchen with hands still grubby. Mother said, "Beth, as long as you wish to have dirty hands, you are not prepared to enter the kitchen." She returned well scrubbed. Same procedure the next day, same procedure again until she got all her dresses back.

This certainly was a game of mutual retaliation: Beth's dress was dirty, so her mother took her other dresses away; Beth refused to wash her hands and was told to leave the table; Beth went to the kitchen with dirty hands and was evicted. The consequences imposed on Beth were logical but ineffective since they were used in a power conflict; thus they settled nothing and led to more provocation and defiance. Where did the mother fail?

It was a logical consequence to deprive Beth of clean dresses as long as she was getting them dirty. Mother was right in stating that if Beth did not care how she looked, neither did she. But did the mother really mean it? Her act of removing the dresses from the closet was hostile, committed on the spur of the moment when she was angry and trying to punish Beth. Logical consequences work only if each step is taken without anger and malice.

RESPONSIBILITY FOR CLOTHES, TOYS, BOOKS

A distressing shortcoming of children is their negligence and carelessness with their belongings. Few parents know how to cope with the problem; consequently, when provoked, they usually respond quickly and impulsively.

Most parents cannot stand a blatant disregard of order. Most family discussions—or more correctly arguments—will be directed at transgressions of orderliness. It is in this area that the application of logical consequences is most essential. Herbert Spencer, who about one hundred years ago described the effectiveness of logical consequences, suggested a corrective procedure to replace the prevalent application of punishment.

> Having refused or neglected to pick up and put away the things that children scattered about and thereby having entailed the trouble of doing this on someone else, the child should, on subsequent occasions, be denied the means of giving this trouble. When it next petitions for the toy box, the reply of its Mama should be, "The last time you had your toys, you left them lying on the floor, and Jane had to pick them up. Jane is too busy to pick up every day the things you leave around, and I cannot do it myself, so if you will not put your toys away when you are done with them, I cannot let you have them."

Parents have discovered many arrangements which impress the child as a logical consequence of his negligence and induced him to mend his ways without feeling subdued or imposed upon. It it the pressure of reality that exerts the greatest influence on the child. But one must be careful to avoid anger or a spirit of retaliation, or the application of logical consequences will fail.

There is value in giving a child a deadline so as to avoid daily conflicts and to create a solution once a week. However, the report below raises some questions about the adequacy of deadlines.

> Every Saturday morning the house was a battleground. Scott, age 5, did not want to pick up the toys which had accumulated in his room during the week. He wanted to go outside and play or watch TV. Mother told him it was up to him. If he didn't want to pick up the toys, it was all right. However, if he wanted to play outside or watch TV, the toys would first have to be picked up. The first two Saturdays it took Scott a long time finally to decide to tidy up his room. After that, it was usually done right away so that he could then play.

First of all, why should the toys lay around for a whole week? Also, in saying that Scott picks up his toys on Saturday, why usually "right away"? One has to assume that the mother must remind Scott several times every Saturday about picking up his toys. Such use of logical consequences is not effective.

Here is another situation involving logical consequences where the idea is sound but the execution is not.

> It wasn't too hard to get Neal, age 7, to have a bath or shower every night, but he used to leave a pile of clothes and towels on the floor of the bathroom, and repeated pleas to clean up did not have any effect. He finally let his dirty clothes pile up in a corner of the bathroom for several days until he ran out of clean clothes for the morning. Mother then pointed out, after the moans and groans had subsided, that Neal couldn't really expect to have clean clothes if he didn't put the dirty clothes down the laundry chute to be washed.

> A month later, Neal fairly consistently put clothes down the chute. He still didn't hang his towels up, but at least there was a big improvement.

Parents who use logical consequences often succeed up to a certain point, but cannot stay out of the struggle completely. If Neal is only "fairly" consistent in disposing of his dirty clothes, he is still waiting to be reminded by mother. And why can't he take care of his towels as well as his clothes? Since there is no benefit in his being negligent (he cannot enjoy drying himself with a dirty towel), one has to assume Neal is misbehaving to get special attention from his mother. From what the child is doing, one can always clearly see what the parents are doing. It belongs together, like two parts of a dialogue.

In the following example it is clear that action was taken without a lot of talking and reminding. This makes the consequence effective.

> A family had been having trouble with many items left out of place through-
> out the home. At a family meeting it was decided that each night before
> going to bed, each member of the family should check to make sure that all
> of his or her possessions had been put away properly. If any item was left
> out of place, such as a book which belonged in a bookcase, in a bedroom
> (and not on the family room floor), or a coat which belonged in the closet
> (not left over a chair), then that item was picked up by the mother and put
> in a box in the parents' bedroom. Any item put in the box was not returned
> to the owner until the next Sunday at the next regular family council meet-
> ing. After that decision, only rarely did an item have to be put away.

Here is a nice little twist to the same procedure, proving that parents and children can be quite ingenious in developing techniques of applying logical consequences.

> In a family of four children, each was responsible for keeping his clothes
> hung up and in order. Due to laxity, however, something had to be done.
> Mother called a family council meeting and suggested they have a nickel
> basket. All clothes or other misplaced articles were to be placed in the basket
> and could be removed only after paying a nickel fine for each article, and
> they all had to be reclaimed simultaneously. The children heartily accepted
> the idea.

> At first the basket was full. One girl was wearing the same skirt for a week
> because the rest were in the basket and she didn't want to spend the money
> to retrieve them. However, in a few weeks all learned the lesson, and the
> basket remained empty. It took only a few more weeks for the basket to go
> out of existence.

Let us compare this procedure with another reported by a mother.

> In the home there was a rule that all clothes put in the wash must be right
> side out, all buttons undone, and all pockets empty. If the rule was not fol-
> lowed, the logical consequences were that the owner of the clothes must wash
> them himself.

The spirit of this report is like a military command: all clothes "must be," and the owner of the clothes "must wash them himself." Such com-
mands are sufficient to disqualify the example as an application of logical consequences. The mother could have said that she was not willing to wash

clothes if the right side was not out, the buttons undone, and the pockets emptied; then it would be up to the owner to decide what to do. If he wanted his clothes washed, he would have to do it himself. But in the situation presented, if the negligent child refused to wash his own clothes, the result would be harsh words, tears, and hard feelings.

Here is a typical example of how logical consequences can lead to a power struggle.

> Ralph, age 8, left his good clothes strewn all around the room. Mother had been trying for a long time to get him to pick up his things. Exasperated, she took all clothes which were lying around and put them away. The following Sunday Ralph couldn't find his good clothes. "Hey, where is my Sunday suit?" When told that it had been put away and that he would have to go to Sunday school in school clothes, he burst into a temper tantrum. "I have told you and told you to hang up your things, Ralph. Now let this be a lesson to you." "Then I won't go to Sunday school," Ralph screamed. "Oh, yes you will. Now get dressed. You haven't much time." "I won't, I won't, I won't." Mother finally gave up the fight with Ralph, who refused to dress. "Well, will you promise to hang them up when you get home, if I give your clothes back to you?" "Sure." Mother returned the clothes and Ralph rushed into them. When he got back, he left them strewn around as usual.

The mother's actions clearly indicate her effort to overpower Ralph. And, as usual, he won out and she gave in. All basic principles of conflict solving were violated. First, mother both fought and gave in. Second, she did not recognize the real issue. It was not whether Ralph would have his Sunday suit; it was a question of personal involvement, of who would win and who would lose. Third, the mother was unconsciously agreeing with Ralph to serve him if he would fight long and hard enough. She did not realize she could change the agreement if she changed her role in the game, which was fighting. Finally, there was no mutual decision making, no shared responsibility; the mother decided single-handedly after getting angry.

Since disorder is an expression of rebellion, it infuriates a mother. But as long as she continues to fight, there is no chance for improvement. The following example shows the kind of impasse reached in many families.

> Grace, age 9, sat at the desk in the living room. Wilma, age 7, was on the floor, cutting out paper dolls. Scraps of paper lay all around. "Clean up when you are finished, girls," mother commented as she passed through the living room. "We will," Wilma answered with heavy disgust. Her face had an expression that signified "Here we go again!" The next time mother went through the living room, both girls were watching TV. The desk was a mess of papers, and the scraps and paper dolls lay all over the floor. "Be sure to clean up, girls," mother admonished again. "Yes, Mother," came the chorus

automatically. A little later mother noticed that the girls had a snack and had left their glasses on top of the TV set. "For heaven's sake, will you pick up after yourselves? Look at the mess you have made!" "All right, Mother," said Grace in an exasperated voice, "we will."

Not long after this, mother found Grace lying on her bed reading, and Wilma outside playing. The living room was a shambles. She called Wilma and burst forth angrily, "Get busy and clean up. We have company coming for dinner; you know I want this room to look decent. Why can't you pick up when you are through? Before you go on to something else, you should put away what you have been doing. You know that." On and on mother went with her angry preaching. Grace and Wilma sullenly gathered up their things and put them away while mother hovered over them.

There is not the slightest evidence of mutual respect in this situation; both parties show their contempt. The mother has no right to force her concept of order on the girls any more than she is obliged to pick up after them, run after them, and allow them to put her into their service. What she must do to gain her daughters' respect is to determine always what *she* will do. The best way for a mother to discourage disobedience in a child is to be able to say No. She can be successful if she does not talk, if she uses quiet action instead. As long as she talks, she succumbs to the fight.

What could the mother in the above example do? There was no need to tell the girls what to do—they already knew—and their mother really did not expect them to listen. As soon as the girls began watching TV, action was needed. The mother should have turned off the set and made sure it was not turned on before the mess was cleaned up. Furthermore, she should have denied her daughters snacks, drinks, and playtime until they cleaned up the room. In such a situation, if the mother remains calm, firm, and quiet, the girls will probably cooperate. The danger is getting involved in an argument, because the girls will try to "talk themselves out" of the obligation to clean up. Most parents fall for verbal provocations and let themselves get involved in fruitless argument.

A mother's refusal to talk to her son in the example below deprives him of the advantage of being negligent.

Johnny would never put anything in its proper place; he was always forgetting where he put it. As soon as he came home from school, he put his books in the first convenient place he could find; his toys were strewn all over the house, and his clothes were always on the bedroom floor. All the scoldings and threats on mother's part did no good at all. Mother finally got fed up with spending all day picking up after him in vain, and she told him that she no longer would pick up any of his belongings.

Apparently Johnny expected mother to continue picking up after him, because he continued his untidiness. In a few days he began to complain about not being able to find anything, and he demanded to know where his things were. Mother told him that it was now his responsibility to be sure to put things in a place where he would remember. After a few times when he really could not find what he wanted, he became careful and orderly.

What matters here is not that Johnny could not find what he wanted, but that his mother refused to be his slave and take care of his belongings.

Sometimes parents discover drastic ways to make the child aware of the benefits of order.

> Ruth, age 8, had toys and clothes scattered all over the floor. Father and mother decided to let all their clothes and whatever work equipment, books, or dishes they had used lay around wherever they had left them. Their small apartment became so cluttered that there was not even room on the dining-room table to have dinner. When Ruth became hungry, mother said that she was also hungry, but did not offer any solution to the problem. After a puzzled silence, Ruth recognized that there was no room on the table; so she went ahead on her own and cleared a space on the table so the family could eat. After a few days Ruth became quite upset about the disorder and asked her mother to help her clean up everything. From then on she became quite orderly without any further prodding or discussion.

HOUSEHOLD CHORES

Putting one's things away is only one area in which the child contributes to the family welfare. By and large, we find parents taking on all responsibility for the adequate functioning of the family, and consequently, children feel free to do as they please. These same parents, when they try to enforce ideas of order and contributions on their children, find themselves on the losing end. They need to learn how to stimulate the children to observe order and take on responsibility. The way to do this is not to teach children responsibility but to give it to them. This means that parents share their responsibilities. In the situation below the child learns a lesson which very few children experience: that order exists for their benefit as well as for other members of the family.

> Johnny, who not only refused to take care of his belongings and his room but also refused to take on any obligation for the family, made a typical disdainful remark when mother asked him to take out the garbage, as he had promised he would. "Gee, why do I always have to do something?" Whereupon, mother invited him to have a little chat. "How would you like it if for a whole week you could do whatever you wanted, without any duties?" He could hardly believe such a proposal. Of course he would like

it. (This is the dream of every red-blooded American boy, to be able to do as he pleases.) "Do you really mean it? I would not need to put anything away? I would not have to wash my hands before coming to the table? I would not have to take a bath, or carry out the garbage?" Mother agreed: "If you would like to do that for a week, it would be all right with me. But there is one condition." (Johnny knew there must be a hitch somewhere; it was too good to be true.) "If you can do that, then I should have the right to do the same; don't you think so?" What a silly question, Johnny thought. Mother always does what she wants anyhow; why should she need special permission for that? So they both agreed, and the boy went happily to bed looking forward to a week of complete freedom.

Next morning when he came to the breakfast table, there was no breakfast waiting for him. He called to his mother, who was still in bed, asking about his breakfast. Mother told him she didn't feel like getting up to make breakfast; he could help himself if he wanted to. It was not too pleasant getting his own breakfast, but a small price to pay for his freedom, Johnny thought. When he came for lunch, nothing was prepared. Mother told him that she was going out to have lunch with a friend. And for the rest of the day, whenever something needed to be done, mother was busy with something else. She did not feel like driving Johnny to a boy scout meeting, or sewing on a button, or pressing his clothes, and so on.

One of the most disliked household chores is washing the dishes. Nobody wants to do it. Usually a mother feels that if she has cooked the meal, set the table, and cleared it, she has worked enough. In the example below the mother attempts to apply a logical consequence which proves ineffective.

Gloria was asked to finish doing the dinner dishes and to put them away before she did her homework or had a friend over for the evening. Mother and father left for an evening class and returned home to find the kitchen as they had left it. Though Gloria enjoyed sleeping as late as possible in the morning, the next morning she was awakened ten minutes early. This gave her ample time to take care of the dishes so that breakfast could be prepared in the kitchen. This was a logical consequence for Gloria's behavior which had disrupted the social order of the home. Her individual procedure was disrupted in order to permit the morning routine for the whole family.

The consequence might have been effective, because it certainly was unpleasant for Gloria. Furthermore, the mother's position was clear and natural: Gloria disrupted the order of the family; therefore the family has the right to disrupt her personal order. However, the mother's action was strictly retaliatory; there was no effort made to reach an agreement.

Here is an example which requires careful evaluation as to the use of consequences.

> In a family everyone had certain jobs at dinnertime—setting the table, clearing it, or washing the dishes. Sue, the youngest, age 9, refused to do her job. In a family council it was decided that she could not eat with the family if she did not want to do her job. She ate at a separate table at a different time. Each day she was given the choice of doing her job or eating by herself. She chose to eat alone, which she did for about a week. She finally decided she wished to join the family and do her job. Never again did Sue fail to do it.

Using the four principles of conflict solving in a democratic transaction, one can determine what is correct and incorrect; this example shows a peculiar mixture of both. Instead of daily bickering, reminding, and coaxing, a certain procedure was decided upon by the family. The consequence was arranged so that it was always up to Sue to decide whether she wanted to conform. But then the question arises: Was the issue recognized? And did Sue participate in decision making? It is obvious that Sue was involved in a power conflict. Not only did she refuse to do what was expected of her; even when the consequence was invoked with its unpleasant effects, Sue suffered the consequence rather than give in. It took her a whole week to realize that the family would not yield and it was silly to continue a useless fight. She gave in because the family refused to be involved. But the imposition of a consequence was obviously a punitive, retaliatory act on the part of the family. This was a forceful way to show her that she did not belong to the family if she did not do her job. However, the redeeming feature in this application of consequences was letting Sue make the decision about whether to eat with the family. She understood the conditions under which she could rejoin the family.

In our cultural setting parents tend to burden themselves with responsibility. Even those parents who want sincerely to get out of the struggle, and would like to let the situation exert its influence, flounder and continue to be involved. One has to be exceedingly careful not to fall for the temptation of domination.

> Dolores, Joanne, and Barbara, ages 10, 11, and 12, agreed that each would do the dishes for one meal a day during the summer vacation. At first they did fine and rotated the breakfast, lunch, and dinner chores. But soon they began to put off longer and longer doing the dishes, until those from the last meal were not clean when it was time for the next meal. The family discussed the problem and decided that the person responsible for the previous meal's unwashed dishes must also take on the next meal's dishes, since it was impossible to tell which girl was responsible for each meal. (It was not possible to use the natural consequences of not being able to

cook the next meal when the dishes were dirty, as the girls knew that during the school year, when mother took the responsibility for the dishes, she usually did them only once a day.) There was no more dallying involving the dishwashing.

Again we can see how close mother came to sharing responsibility but could not quite make it. Her overprotection of the children is quite obvious. Why couldn't the girls be responsible for dishes during the school year? Why couldn't the mother let the girls experience the impact of their negligence without interfering? After all, it was not up to her to bring about a solution; if the girls were dissatisfied with their performance, it would be up to them to decide what to do. The arrangement that each girl responsible for the last meal's dishes would, if the dishes had not been washed, take on the next meal's dishes was arbitrary. Somebody is sitting in judgment. And yet, despite all these flaws, the procedure succeeded because a new routine was established which excluded arguing and bickering. This is essential for the successful application of consequences.

Lisbeth, age 15, loved to cook and bake. She did both well. It was a great help to mother since she did not return from work until after 5:00 P.M.

However, once the mixing and baking were over, the dirty dishes became a giant chore to Lisbeth. If mother continued to remind her, she would put the dishes to soak in the sink, but found it difficult to wash, dry, and put them away. Mother soon realized that nagging and reporting to daddy would do no good. She felt she had several ways of handling the problem. First, she could leave the dishes in the sink and prepare the other meals around them. (This didn't seem to be the beginning of a happy mealtime.) Second, she could offer to help Lisbeth do the dishes. (Mother felt Lisbeth would never learn to do them on her own, and mother would become part of her scheme.) Third, mother could refuse Lisbeth the use of the kitchen. Fourth, mother could ask for a family meeting to discuss the matter and see what solutions could be drawn out.

There was a family meeting where the problem and possible solutions were discussed. All the family members wanted Lisbeth to continue to bake since the results were so pleasing. She said she hadn't realized how concerned mother was with the messy kitchen. She asked to be permitted to continue baking and cooking and felt it was best if she cleaned up immediately.

Next time Lisbeth baked, the cake was beautiful, but the messy mixer stood by the cake along with the dirty dishes. Mother reminded her of the family decision. She said she was planning to clean up "in just a minute." In the meantime mother fixed the rest of the meal.

When it was time for dessert, mother brought in fruit and cookies. Lisbeth was confused and disappointed when her cake was not offered. Mother told Lisbeth she had decided to have the other dessert, because Lisbeth had not carried out her part of the bargain. No more was said.

Several days later Lisbeth began baking again. After the cookies were made, she washed, dried, and put away all the bowls and pans. She made sure her dessert would be served at the evening meal.

All this happened several years ago. Although the final outcome succeeded (Lisbeth now loves to cook and cleans up willingly), the mother now sees the steps she should have taken. It was her decision, not the family's, when she substituted another dessert for the cake. She used punishment by withholding the cake.

The mother caught one mistake, but there were many others. First of all, she asked for a family meeting to discuss Lisbeth's problem, but it is not the function of the family meeting to be called when something goes wrong. Family meetings should be held regularly, not just when a parent is angry about a particular situation. Second, there was no need to remind Lisbeth of the family decision. Third, working around the dishes, as the mother chose to do, was wrong: the natural consequence of an untidy kitchen with unwashed dishes is that it cannot be used. Fourth, it may not be evident to Lisbeth that because she cooks she must wash dishes; does her mother always do the dishes when she cooks? Lisbeth should be presented with two alternatives in a family council: either she bakes and cleans up, or she does not bake at all. Once a decision is made—in this instance Lisbeth's accepting the responsibility for washing the dishes after baking—nothing should be said until the next family council. This would be the democratic procedure, with the consequences of a neglected responsibility obvious to the whole family. Then Lisbeth would recognize the consequences and act accordingly. A final question remains: Why did a faulty procedure have good results? It was not merely the arbitrary punishment. There was a saving grace in the mother's action. She acted without talking. And it is the absence of words which impresses children.

Children can be influenced in many ways to assume responsibility whether for doing dishes or other household duties. Refusal to cook when the dishes are unwashed and the kitchen dirty is one of the simplest ways to impress children with the logic of the situation. In the following example we see a peculiar twist to the method.

Through use of the family council, a system of dividing up chores was arranged. In most instances Sally and Gloria seemed to fulfill their assignments reasonably well, except for clearing the table and dishwashing, which they both disliked. Since this task usually came up just as their favorite TV programs were on, they hit on the scheme of doing their chores during the commercials and station breaks. This sometimes found them still unfinished by bedtime, and more than once mother had to remind them to complete the task before going to bed.

After thinking it over and discussing it with her husband, who was agreeable to the experiment, mother decided to take a leaf from her daughters' book and cook dinner during the commercials. She took the evening when her favorite programs were on, and, as it happened, there were three in a sequence. Though the children complained about being hungry, mother did not answer them, except to say that she was preparing the meal as fast as she could under the circumstances. At ten thirty dinner was finally ready. After that there were very few lapses on completing the dishes as soon as subsequent dinners were finished.

The mother's idea here is good but flawed. Why did she have to remind Sally and Gloria to complete the task before going to bed? She taught them a lesson, but only once; as a consequence, there were still lapses on taking care of the dishes. Though the mother was moving in the right direction, replacing her nagging with quiet action, she was still involved.

Mother had established a pattern of spending most of Saturday nagging the children to do the tasks that had been set for each of them in the family council. Realizing what she was doing, she brought up this matter at the next family council, saying that the nagging was wearing her down; it created much friction in the family. She asked if the family could jointly find a solution to the problem. After much discussion, it was decided that the responsibility should not even be mentioned by mother, but that all tasks must be finished by four o'clock every Saturday. The children were free to choose when on Saturday, in the morning or afternoon, they would take care of their tasks.

The following Saturday three of the children went merrily about doing their jobs. Jim, the fourth child, decided to play basketball with his buddies. Then he watched a TV program until lunch. He had been the one whom mother had to nag the most, but this time she said nothing. At 2 P.M. mother and father decided to take the children to the beach for a few hours. Much to Jim's dismay, he was unable to join them because he still had the lawn to mow. He asked if he could wait and mow the lawn on Monday after school; but the decision of the family council held. He stayed home and cut the grass while the family went to the beach. The following Saturday, and thereafter, Jim made sure he completed his task before he played basketball and watched TV.

Here we can see that the mother really shared her responsibility with the family. She brought her problem to the family council and asked for help in finding a solution. The crucial phrase is "*it* was decided," rather than "*we* decided."

A frequent source of conflict is the unwillingness of many children to clean up their rooms. They consider the task an imposition. There are many ways by which parents are able to promote willingness to keep a room tidy.

Jan and her sister Sally shared the same bedroom. Both girls had been encouraged to make their own beds and to keep their room neat. Sally had done quite well and was even willing to tidy up the entire room. But she refused to make Jan's bed when Jan wasn't interested in doing her share. This led to almost daily quarreling. Mother and father believed this was a power contest with them as well as a display of sibling rivalry. Feeling inadequate in competition with her sister, Jan resorted to negative behavior.

As Jan had on occasion gone to school with her bed unmade, mother decided to give both girls a choice. She discussed with them the necessity for having to share the same room, and the responsibility of each in sharing their duties. Since the bedmaking seemed to be the central source of conflict, the discussion was soon centered on this point. Mother suggested that since there was the bedmaking problem, perhaps something should be done about it. Mother asked the girls whether they would rather have their beds unmade during the day, or would they rather make them? Both girls decided to leave their beds unmade. After they had left for school, their mother and father folded the spreads, blankets, and sheets, and stacked them by the foot of the beds. Mother later explained to them that they had chosen to leave their beds unmade—it was their room to keep as they saw fit. Both girls promptly made their beds.

The following morning both beds were made before the girls left for school. Two mornings later Sally made hers but Jan did not. Mother removed Jan's covers and put them on the floor. When Jan returned from school she was again upset by the procedure. She promptly made her bed and after that had it made each morning before going to school. Even though the room was not what one could call shipshape, the parents made it a point to praise the girls for their efforts.

The interesting feature of this example is the extreme to which the parents take the girls' decision in favor of unmade beds. Because the parents acted quickly, and there were no angry words, the procedure proved effective.

The situation below is similar to ones discussed before, in which the logic of the family's action is questionable.

Fred, age 9, refused to keep his room clean. He neither made his bed nor put his things away, so one could not enter his room without stepping on something. After endless fights and threats, which of course were useless, it was decided to institute a family council. To be sure, Fred's untidiness was only one of the many problems that had to be faced and dealt with. In discussing Fred's right to have his room untidy, the council came to the conclusion that it was up to him if he wanted to have his room like a pigsty. But since he chose to have it this way, the family decided that they could then dump anything lying around elsewhere in his room. At first it did not seem to affect him in any way, but after a few weeks he felt so uncomfortable in his room that he asked for help in cleaning it up. From then on he was more careful.

More perceptive and respectful parents could have avoided this experience for Fred. His mother could have refused to change his linens if his room and bed were in disorder. Or the mother could have offered to help Fred clean up his room on the weekend, so that with new linens, the room would begin in a tidy fashion every week.

Even though Fred is granted the right to keep his room as he wants it, none of the rest of the family should necessarily have the right to add to Fred's mess. However, because the family's action was carried out quietly and eliminated arguing, coaxing, and threatening, it proved effective.

EATING

Many parents take for granted the fact that many children refuse to eat; this is absurd. There are probably no other living beings on earth who refuse to take nourishment except our children. They prefer to starve if they can obtain the special attention of their parents. The natural consequence of a child's refusal to eat is that he will be hungry; and most parents will play right into the child's hands at that point.

> Eric, age 7, a middle child, was a very finicky eater. As daddy served generous portions of beef stew—a family favorite—Eric slumped down in his chair and petulantly said, "I don't like any of that stuff." "Eric, please try it," mother pleaded. "You know I don't like things all mixed up together," Eric whined. "I simply won't eat it." "Well, all right, I'll fix you a hamburger." While mother prepared the food, Eric played with his knife. Father and the other children finished their meal and left the table, while mother stayed with Eric, who slowly finished his hamburger.

This is a typical procedure. The mother has not succeeded in making the child eat; rather, the child has succeeded in putting mother into his service and making *her* do for him what he wants. The only effective response to a child who is a poor eater is to leave him strictly alone.

> Danny, age 9, was a very poor eater. He took minimal amounts of food and spent hours before he got it down, while mother coaxed and pushed. When she came for consultation it was explained to her that Danny would not eat as long as she was more interested in his intake of food than he was. It was not easy to convince her that she should leave him alone and

merely put the food in front of him. When she returned two weeks later she reported that nothing had changed. This sounded rather improbable, because most children begin to eat when mothers stay away. And then it was discovered that mothers can shout with their mouths closed.

As long as not eating will pay off for Danny, he will continue to disdain food. Poor eaters always have parents who are interested in their eating. In the above case the mother maintained her concern although she did not say anything.

Tony was invited to a party. Apparently he was a very poor eater. All the children had finished, but Tony still had his whole cup of cocoa and chewed away on a sandwich without noticeable effect. His grandmother who was with him remarked that it often took him an hour to finish his meal. She tried to persuade him, "Aren't you ashamed, Tony? All the others have almost finished. Hurry up." The hostess asked her to leave the room and then turned to the boy. "At our house you don't have to eat if you don't want to. Give me your cup and your sandwich." She made a gesture of taking them away. At once Tony grabbed them with both hands, and took a huge bite of the sandwich. Now he had both cheeks full, but he could not get the food down. His training was against him. She persisted, "No, that won't do. I can tell you are not hungry. So I will just take the food away from you *if* you don't want to eat it." Nothing more was said. Within five minutes the cocoa was gone and the sandwich consumed, to the great amazement of the grandmother, who could not understand how the feat had been accomplished.

Tony did not dislike eating; but he insisted on eating on his own terms, which meant keeping his grandmother, and probably his mother, busy. But this does not mean that he would let anybody else take the food away from him. Poor eaters, particularly those who use mealtime for tyrannizing adults, feel honor bound to hang on to their food when somebody threatens to take it away from them. This paradox can be observed with children who do not eat much for a long period of time. Physicians are inclined to consider this difficulty an illness which they call *anorexia nervosa*. They suggest all kinds of treatment, often without result. A doctor's inability to understand the reasons for a child's not eating prevents him from using effective consequences which could stimulate the child's interest in food. It takes considerable courage and conviction to be aware of a child's detrimental attitude toward food rather than his "need" for food. One of the worst cases was the following.

John was seven years old when his mother brought him to our summer camp. He had just recovered from whooping cough. He coughed and vomited not only when he started to eat, but also when he became excited or exerted himself physically. He had lost so much weight that he was down to skin and bones. The frantic parents had hired a nurse who fed him several times a day. Each feeding took hours. The nurse had literally to force each bite into his mouth. The result was that he swallowed a small amount of food, but most of the time it did not stay down.

I was willing to accept the boy on the condition that the parents would not visit him for two weeks and would not inquire about his loss or gain of weight. The parents had already tried everything else; they had no alternative except to agree. The boy actually ate nothing for a few days. When food was placed before him, he just looked at it. Nobody made any remarks (a rule which was difficult to enforce). After a little while the plate was removed and, according to the rules, nothing else was offered to him. He took only milk and fluids when they were served to all children. It was difficult to watch this child starve himself without doing something about it—but it was the only way to cure him. Some of the women workers in the camp actually could not stand it and tried to give him some extra food. I had to threaten to fire anyone who would do so. And the plan paid off.

Toward the end of the first week John started to put some food into his mouth. The following anecdote describes the way he did it. We had taken an excursion. I encountered John after about an hour of the hike and asked him how he was. He did not answer. This was puzzling, as he generally was a friendly boy. I tried to find out what was troubling him, but was unable to get any response. Finally I asked him to open his mouth. He obliged. There was a bun which he had taken at breakfast more than an hour earlier. He had put it in his mouth, but had neither chewed nor swallowed it. It took two weeks of patient waiting before he started to eat normally. But then all difficulties were gone and he gained weight very rapidly.

The first prerequisite to helping children change their minds and intentions is to not be deceived by their mistaken goals. The quiet firmness—without fighting or giving in—made the child realize the futility of his efforts.

One must keep in-mind the physiological reaction to being forced to eat. The stomach is not ready to take in food if its digestive function is disturbed. Conversely, removing the pressure of food intake can stimulate the flow of gastric juices. The following episode demonstrates this fact.

Eva, age 4, did not feel like eating her evening meal. Instead of trying to talk her into it, we told her that she does not have to eat anything. However, she would not get the piece of chocolate which was usually given to her before going to bed. She sat there, thinking it over. Then she asked whether she could try again. Of course she could. After she took a few bites she suddenly exclaimed, "Isn't it funny, suddenly it doesn't taste so bad anymore."

Many children decide they will eat only one kind of food, as in the following example.

Max, age 9, refused to take any food except hot dogs. Every mealtime was a fight to get a few bites of food down his throat. Then mother was advised to make a deal with Max. Would he like to have hot dogs for every meal for a whole week? He was delighted at such a prospect. So mother gave him hot dogs for breakfast, lunch, and dinner, and nothing else. He enjoyed it—for three days. Then he had enough of hot dogs and wanted other food. Mother remained firm, which is not easy for a mother to do. She refused to give him anything but hot dogs for the rest of the week. Thereafter Max ate everything.

Similar procedures can be employed whenever a child imposes restrictions on food. Some children may decide to take only fluids. This is usually the consequence of mother's trying to impose on the child the intake of solids. It may take some time before the child will give up his food restriction, but he will do so if the parents refrain from putting on any pressure. As was said before, this is extremely difficult for many mothers to do because they are concerned with a proper, well-balanced diet. Similarly, children may refuse to eat any food that is not "pure," that is, food containing various ingredients.

All such tactics have to be understood as part of a power struggle in which mother and child are involved. It makes little difference whether the child eats too little or too much, whether he is too slow or eats too fast; everything he does is an invitation to, and a consequence of, a struggle. The crucial question is: Who wins?

Henry was a finicky eater. At breakfast he picked at his food and complained because the cereal was not to his liking. At lunch he ate only a peanut-butter-and-jelly sandwich, and at dinner, potatoes and dessert. Trying everything else, mother finally hit on the idea of merely putting the food provided on the table and taking it off whether he had finished it or not. Though he complained bitterly the first two days, it was not long before he was eating most of the regular foods which were presented to him.

What can one do if other members of the family do not adhere to the principle of non-involvement? The father or a grandmother might continue the fuss and pressure, even though mother may have succeeded in staying apart from the struggle. However, for the child it is important what *mother* does. Regardless of what other members of the family may do, the mother can establish between herself and the child a not-fighting, not-giving-in relationship of mutual respect. But how can she sit by quietly when other members of the family reject her plea? The mother must influence the members of the family in the same way she influences the child. When grandmother still coaxes little John to eat, despite the mother's appeal not to, mother can quietly take her plate and go to another room to eat. One can be reasonably sure that grandmother will not like this; she then has to decide whether she wants to continue to behave in such a way that mother will not eat with the family. All disturbances around the dinner table can be resolved in a similar way.

It is amazing how close mothers come to applying logical consequences correctly and at the last moment violate the principle and undo what they have achieved. The example below is important because it shows clearly what should and should not be done. More significant, it pinpoints the reason why the mother did not follow through.

> Fred, age 4, did not sit in the chair at the dinner table. He sat on his knees, off to one side, stood, walked around, and invariably spilled something in the process. This was probably an attention-getting device, since he could not generally take part in the conversation.
>
> One day Fred again behaved in this way, and mother asked him whether he wanted to sit in the chair the right way, or if he would rather not have the chair and stand up; so he moved his chair back and continued eating. Not more than five minutes went by before he asked to have his chair again. He was told that he could not have it back for this meal, but had to continue eating standing up, since that was what he wanted. He cried a little but continued eating, with the rest of the family not paying any attention to his crying. At the next meal Fred asked if he could sit in his chair, and he was told that he could if he remembered that he had to sit quietly. A gentle reminder during that meal was enough to keep him in his seat. (The others also included him in the conversation at the table.) His behavior since then generally improved, though occasional reminders were necessary. Part of the problem may involve the restlessness common to this age.

In the moment when reminding is necessary, Fred indicates that he has not learned to take responsibility for himself. Whether the reminding is gentle or not makes little difference; it is wrong. But why does the mother persist? Fortified by so-called research of the experts, many people believe that children are not able to sit quietly for any length of time. This mother believed in the "restlessness common to this age"; others assume that a child has too much energy. (Hyperactivity is frequently attributed to "minimal brain damage," regardless of whether such an assumption is verified or not, and in most cases it is not.) Logical consequences make sense only when one believes the child can learn from them, that he can change his behavior if he decides to do so. Any assumption of a child's inability to behave and to function indicates widespread pessimism toward and distrust of a child. We generally underestimate the child's ability to decide his own behavior.

It is questionable whether this arrangement of letting Fred stand up to eat was the best his mother could do. If standing up is the consequence, then one would always have to give the child a new choice, or else go around the table and remove the child who, at the moment of pending deprivation of his chair, would probably sit in it. The most effective technique, and the one most frequently used, is to quietly remove the child's plate as soon as he plays with his food, eats with his hands, does not sit properly, dawdles, or otherwise misbehaves. He is told he does not get another chance to eat until the next meal, regardless of how much he may cry, throw a temper tantrum, or promise to be "good." If a young child becomes aggressive, destructive, or has a temper tantrum, one can remove him quietly, but not without giving him a choice; he may return to the table when he is willing to behave. He is not "punished" for what he has done, but merely excused *as long as* he does not want to behave. If he refuses to leave, one can let him decide whether he wants to leave by himself or be carried out. For an adult such a choice often appears insignificant; he sees only the fact that the child is forced to leave. But it makes all the difference to the child whether he is asked to leave or given a choice as to how he will leave.

Removal of the plate is also a logical consequence if a child has difficulty coming to the table. It is never necessary to call a child for meals more than once. However, most parents have an unspoken agreement with children whereby calling them once is understood as insignificant. Many parents train their children to come only when they yell.

> One of the most distressing transgressions of Bob, age 11, was his refusal to come on time for dinner. The father did everything, including using his belt. Nothing helped. Bob never came on time. I tried to explain to the father the reason for the boy's behavior. Bob obviously defeated a very domineering father who simply could not stand his son's defiance. All the father needed to do was to refuse to serve Bob when he came late. The father could not accept that. He maintained one should not deprive a child of his food. It was explained to him that it was not he who deprived Bob of his food, but Bob himself, by his refusal to come to dinner on time. After long persuasion and a short discussion with Bob, it was agreed that no dinner would be served to him if he came late.
>
> Two weeks later the father came again, and reported that "it did not work."

I could hardly believe it. Did Bob continue to come late? "Yes." Did he get any meal then? "Definitely not." It didn't make sense to me: a healthy boy not coming to dinner and getting no food! So I asked the father whether he really did not get anything to eat. At that point the father got rather angry, saying he had already told me so. Then I ventured a guess. Did he get anything before he went to bed? "Of course," said the father. "One can't let a child go to bed hungry."

Here we see clearly the consequence of the deep sense of responsibility. This case was in Vienna. In the United States the mother would most likely seek counsel rather than the father; American mothers take on full responsibility so that neither husbands nor children have to do it. It is this exaggerated sense of responsibility which prevents mothers from letting the child experience the consequences at the right moment. It breaks the mother's heart when her child suffers or is deprived of something.

If a child comes to the table with dirty hands, a fight is on too, whether his mother overlooks the hands or makes him wash them. If she ignores the situation, she lets the child defy order; if she orders him to wash, she is imposing her will on the child. What she should do is to refuse to serve him or leave the table. The child has the right to come to the table with dirty hands, but the mother has no obligation to sit at the table with someone who is dirty.

Naturally, all these incidents which can be answered in an immediate way through logical consequences are expressions of a deep-seated struggle, of disturbed relationships. Letting logical or natural consequences take place is only one way—and often the first and most effective way—of dealing with the problem. But it takes more than consequences to overcome the antagonism and hostility that presently exist, either openly or subtly, in our homes.

BRUSHING TEETH

The question of personal hygiene lends itself to conflicts and contests.

Betty, age 3, neglected to brush her teeth. In order to get it done, mother had to go with her and force her each time. The quarrel upset both mother and Betty. The mother thought of a consequence. She told Betty that she need not brush her teeth if she did not want to. But since candy and sweets destroy unbrushed teeth, Betty could have no sweets. Thereafter mother avoided any mention of teeth brushing. For a week Betty neither brushed her teeth nor had any sweets. The other children had candy and ice cream. One afternoon Betty told her mother that she wanted to brush her teeth and have some candy. "Not now, Betty, morning and evening are the times to brush teeth." The girl accepted this without complaint. That evening she brushed her teeth of her own accord.

This is a simple and effective way to impress a child with the consequences of her negligence. Another approach was used with an older girl.

> A girl, at the age of 10, did not want to brush her teeth, regardless of her parents' effort to impress her with the need to do so. Mother told her that if she had more than two cavities, she would have to pay the dentist herself. At the end of the year she had three cavities. She paid seven dollars for filling the third and then started brushing regularly. The mother never nagged her, but stuck to her ultimatum.

Was the above application of consequences in good form? It could have been handled more democratically. It is possible that in a meeting of the family council the children could have come to a conclusion similar to the mother's. Ultimatums can be effective, especially if they imply a choice; yet why were two cavities acceptable but not the third one? Despite the arbitrary establishment of consequences, the fact that nothing was said and the daughter knew what to expect made it an effective procedure.

PUBLIC EMBARRASSMENT

How to behave on the street often causes a major conflict between children and parents.

> Mother and Sharon were on their way home from the playground when Sharon decided she wanted to stop at her auntie's house. Mother said no, they were going home now. Sharon whimpered and begged. Mother continued to walk. The child threw herself on the sidewalk, screaming. Mother calmly and quietly walked on without looking back. Suddenly Sharon jumped up and ran to the mother, smiling and jumping. They walked happily the rest of the way.

A conflict in public, whether on the street, in a supermarket, or a restaurant, embarrasses parents and often results in a decision to yield to the child's demand in order to get the child to cooperate. Parents succumb when their resistance to the child's undue demands and disturbances can be easily undermined.

Once I saw a mother talking to a two-year-old girl who was sitting in the back seat of a car. The mother was pleading with her to come out but the girl refused. What could the mother do? It is so simple. She could have removed the girl from the car without saying anything; after all, it was possible to lift her out. Or she could have walked away, and the girl probably would have followed her, albeit not without screaming. If parents can remain calm without being afraid of what people may say, they usually find children quite willing to follow.

A youngster of three was standing in front of a display window refusing
to budge. His mother and father, who had gone ahead, were shouting at
him, coaxing him. But the boy refused to leave the spot. The parents were
desperate. The father came back and spoke loudly and sharply. The child
pretended not to hear. Finally the father's patience was exhausted. He
grabbed the boy and began to drag him off. And now the real show began.
The child resisted fiercely; he howled and screamed and threw himself on
the sidewalk. Mother and father tugged away at him in great excitement,
until the father picked the boy up bodily and carried him from the battlefield, not at all a radiant victor.

It is so easy to bring a child like this to his senses. There is no need for turmoil or uproar. If the parents had been wise, they would have told the
child after he first refused to move, "You want to look at the show window,
do you? Well, we are sorry but we haven't time. So you'll have to stay by
yourself and we will be going home." When the child sees that they really
mean it, he will not fail to follow. But suppose he had been trained to
defeat his parents, is convinced that in every situation they will give in to
him despite their threats? The parents should then turn at the next corner
and watch their child unseen. When he realizes they are gone, he probably
will run after them. But if not, they can still watch him from a distance,
and follow him if he wanders off. Eventually he will look for them. But it
seldom comes to such an extreme; usually the child learns from being lost.

Leaving a child alone when he has a temper tantrum is sufficient to impress him with its futility. One needs an audience; otherwise the tantrum is
ineffective. Usually parents provide the needed audience. If they fail to do
so, they confront the child with a new reality. He can then adjust to the
needs of the situation. In the following example the boy, when left to his
own resources without his mother or teacher around, becomes ready to
join the others in the group.

One Sunday Terry, age 5, stood in the corner of the Sunday-school classroom crying. Mother coaxed and begged him to stop. "If you don't stop
crying, I am going to go off and leave you." The boy cried louder. "Now
I am really going to go." Terry screamed and edged toward the door after
mother. She slipped out of the door and right back in again when Terry
let out a piercing wail. "Now, Terry, you must stay right here and stop
crying." The teacher stepped in. "Mrs. X, why don't you just go home?
Terry will be all right." "I'm afraid he will leave the church. We had
trouble before we left home." "I am sure Terry will join us when he is
ready. We'll be glad to have you work with us, Terry." Mother left, and
Terry stopped crying but remained in the corner for a while. The teacher
returned to the class. Before long the boy joined the group.

The misbehavior of children in grocery stores and supermarkets has become so common that it is often accepted as normal. Actually, a grocery store is not a playground. Children can learn to understand the difference and behave accordingly.

> George, age 5, climbed over the shopping carts in the supermarket, then scooted onto the rails and sat on the turnstile. "George, get down. You are going to get hurt." The boy ignored mother and hung by his knees from the rail. "Come on, George, get down before you get hurt." Mother pulled a cart from the line. Her son pulled himself up and impishly sat on the turnstile to prevent a woman from coming through. Mother called, "George, get down so the lady can get through." George climbed down, then scrambled up into the carts. "George, come on!" Mother proceeded down the aisle without him. George played on the rails and the turnstiles until his mother had finished shopping and found him so they could leave.

Before entering the store, the mother should have said, "George, the store is not a playground. You may walk down the aisle with me and help get the groceries." If George jumps up into the carts anyway, his mother should immediately lead him by the hand out of the store and to the car saying, "I am sorry you don't feel like behaving in the store. You may wait for me in the car." Or she may interrupt her shopping altogether and take George home, perhaps leaving him at a neighbor's house. Before taking him out again, she should ask whether he is ready to behave. If he creates a disturbance again, he has to stay home a few more times while mother goes shopping, or until he is willing to behave himself.

If one expects the child to behave properly outside the home, one needs to take the time to train at home. Here is an example of a mother's inability to exert any influence.

> Cathy, age 3, refused to stay out of the street when she played outdoors. Mother had to watch her constantly and bring her back from the street. She scolded many times and eventually spanked Cathy without achieving any good results.

What should Cathy's mother have done in this case? Here is an example.

> After many unsuccessful attempts to induce Bob, age 3, not to go out into the street to play, even when other children were doing so, his mother learned in a study group to tell Bob not to go into the street or he would have to come back into the house. Bob went out in the morning to play; after he had been out for about thirty minutes, his mother saw him in the street. She went out and brought him indoors with no talk or anger. Bob complained and cried bitterly. Mother put him in his room until he calmed down. She told him he could try again that afternoon to go out and not play in the street.

This process was repeated approximately five times in three days. After this, a neighbor across the street was amazed to see this three-year-old boy standing on the curb with his arms folded, watching every other child in the neighborhood playing in the street.

It would have been improbable for the boy to respond in this way had the mother shown a punitive, retaliatory attitude. Instead of evoking his defiance, she called him indoors as a logical and acceptable consequence. She spoke to him like a friendly bystander. "He would have to come back" is quite different from "he must" come back. Many children may have difficulty distinguishing a command from an expression of necessity. Parents need to become quite sensitive to subtle changes of expressions which often are of extreme significance.

Children who are at war with their parents will utilize any situation where the parents are vulnerable. If children do not behave properly when the parents entertain guests or visit friends, it is the consequence of their neglect to instill in the children respect for order and people.

Larry, age 6, was a problem to his parents whenever they entertained friends. He would run boisterously around the room and, physically as well as verbally, annoy the visitors. When anything was said to him in an attempt to correct his behavior or to quiet him down, he would retaliate with sarcasm. On one such occasion Larry was sent to his room and was told that when he could conduct himself properly and show respect for other people's feelings, he would be welcome to join the group again. He spent about thirty-five minutes in his room and then returned to join the group. All spent an enjoyable afternoon without further incident.

The above episode is too good to be true. One can assume that Larry liked these particular friends of his parents enough not to want to miss their company. Otherwise a child who is misbehaving to such a degree would not learn respect from such a situation. Then the question is: What should be done if the child refuses to stay in his room? It is usually helpful to have a discussion with the child before the guests arrive. Children should be trained to respect others before they are exposed to them. If need be, the parents can provide the child with an alternative. If he does not behave, he may have to go to his room; if he is not willing to stay in his room, the parents may need a baby-sitter to keep him there. But no decision should be made without agreement with the child; he should be allowed to indicate his preference.

Joan, age 5, was an only child, the only grandchild and the only niece. She and mother were invited to a patio supper next door. Since Joan played with the neighbor girls, Lucy and Mary, a separate table was set up for the children. When they sat down to eat, Joan started to cry. "I want to sit by Mother," she pleaded through her tears. "Now, honey, see how nice it is for you to sit with Lucy and Mary. Come on, eat your supper. Look how good everything is." Joan continued to sob and repeated again and again, "I want to sit by you." Mother became somewhat angry. "I'll take you home if you don't behave." Joan continued to cry. Finally mother gave in, pulled Joan's chair from the children's table, and set it beside hers.

A parent who fights with a child cannot win; he loses even more when the fight occurs in someone else's home. If such disturbances or misbehavior are the rule, one has to take the time and the effort to prepare the child. Furthermore, the mother can arrange with the friends that she will leave immediately when her child begins to misbehave or cause trouble. A few such experiences may make a deep impression on the child.

> Mother's friend dropped in for coffee in the afternoon. As they visited, Mary, the youngest of three, came running in with a tale of injustice from her playmate. Mother commented, "Well, I suppose she doesn't feel well this afternoon." "Why, Mommy?" Mother attempted to answer. Every time mother finished, the child again asked why. Finally mother asked Mary to return to her play so that she could visit. Mary went out but was soon back with more whys. Much of the visit was thus occupied. At last mother admitted to her friend, "That's just her way of getting attention when we have company."

This example illustrates several fundamental problems which the mother recognized partially but was unable to solve. First, the child complained about a playmate; very few parents remain aloof to this bid for attention. They try to explain, suggest, reassure, or they side with the playmate. None of these responses does any good. Siding with the child stimulates him to provoke more unfairness, and taking sides with the opponent (whoever it may be—another child, a teacher, or a member of the family) intensifies his feeling of abusive treatment. The less one says the better; the best response is a sincere "That's too bad." It implies that the child must decide how to resolve his predicament.

Second, the mother realizes the child's effort to get her attention when there is company; Mary is unwilling to share mother with anyone. But how can the mother extricate herself? This brings us to the third problem of the example: what to do when a child asks why. There are two kinds of questions from children which require different adult responses: real questions and silly, attention-getting questions. Real questions deserve sincere explanations and information, except when they pop up when company is around. Then even the honest question should not be answered, but referred to another time when there is a chance to talk things over. When the child asks silly questions, the parent should not answer. If questions are not for the purpose of receiving information, but are asked to keep the adult busy, they can be easily recognized. They fall into the same pattern: "Why, why, why?" "What is this, what is that?" There is no logical link between one silly question and the other; the child may repeat the same question, or raise a new question before the first one is answered. These questions do not require a logical reply but a psychological response. There are many effective forms of declining to become involved, like "that's an interesting question, let's talk about it later," or "what do *you* think?" Or the adult can answer the child with a why of his own before the child has a chance to ask the next question. Changing the subject and talking about something interesting often takes the punch out of the child's behavior. Instead of giving him the desired attention when he misbehaves, one can give him attention in a constructive way, with the intent, however, not to continue it indefinitely. This is one of the areas where a child, through a quiet but firm No, can learn to respect limitations.

One situation in particular is a testing ground for a child's ability to respect order and behave as he knows he should. This is when the family goes to a restaurant. Young children are capable of many tricks to keep parents hopping when dining out; older children can create considerable disturbances too. Again, the family should agree ahead of time on what to do when a child misbehaves in a restaurant. Agreement should be arrived at in the family council. As soon as the disturbance starts in a restaurant, the entire family should go home. One should have a baby-sitter in reserve for such situations; the parents can go out by themselves after taking the children home. The parents should not worry about paying for the uneaten food; it is a small price to pay for having well-behaved children.

In the following example the parents were able to agree on points which usually are controversial and lead to arguments.

> The boys in the family were allowed to order their choice in a restaurant, but the parents noticed that their eyes were bigger than their stomachs. As they sat down to order the next time, the parents told the boys they were still free to order what they wanted but with the understanding that they would eat all of whatever they ordered.

> They ordered excessively just once thereafter, and the parents sat and waited while they finished their meal, although they obviously were not too comfortable. After that, the family never left uneaten food in a restaurant, nor was there ever an argument or unpleasantness when ordering.

> Another problem arose as the boys grew older. The parents noticed that they always ordered the most expensive food. Some means had to be devised to prevent embarrassment when ordering. The parents reached an agreement about how they could avoid humiliating a child or embarrassing

either adult or child. Dad assumed responsibility for looking down the price column and picking a price which the budget could stand. Then he told the children that such and such food sounded good to him. The boys accepted this signal of what should be the top price for a dish, which left them free to choose from a variety of dishes without any fuss or embarrassment.

There may be a slight hint of autocratic control in this example, but the free discussion and sincere agreement about procedure make it a good example of how one can reason with children instead of fighting.

MISCELLANEOUS DAILY OCCURRENCES

There are endless ways a child can disturb his parents when he wants special attention or power over them. And there is an even greater variety of logical consequences possible which parents can learn to apply. To repeat: logical consequences can be effective only if there is no power conflict; certain natural consequences can be applied to any situation.

> Kathie, age 10 months, presented a problem. She had just learned to pull herself to a standing position. She wanted to stand all the time, everywhere. Up to this time, bathtime had been fun for mother and child. Now she wanted to stand in the tub. If she was placed in a sitting position, she would stand up immediately. Besides being dangerous, it was difficult even to wash her. The next bathtime, as soon as she stood up mother said, "It's time to get out," and lifted her from the tub. The next time this procedure was repeated. It took three times, and then there was no problem. Because Kathie enjoyed the tub, this logical consequence worked nicely.

No comment is needed. Obviously, the mother let the logical consequence work for itself without any conflict.

Similar quiet action can be taken when a child does not want to sit down in a stroller. Talking, advising, and scolding are of little value. But the mother can let the child experience the consequence by stopping the stroller until the child sits down, or by taking the child home and not taking him out again until he sits down. This will work with children who fully understand what is said to them and see the connection between standing up and being deprived of going out. With younger children a sudden move of the stroller will let the child fall back on the seat. It usually takes no more than one or two such experiences for the child to realize that sitting down is advisable.

> Kent, age 3, had a great time with his metal cars and trucks; but occasionally his races would end in crashes into the furniture or woodwork. After

having a talk about scratches and dents in the furniture, mother said that the trucks would have to be put away if they knocked into furniture. The next time mother saw them crashing she put them away. After one minute of crying and five of feeling sorry for himself, Kent wanted to know when he could have them back. "As soon as you think you have learned not to let them crash." He said he was ready, and he played with them nicely until bedtime. The next day they crashed. Mother put them away for the day, although Kent said throughout the day that he was ready. By the next day, of course, he *was* ready, and there wasn't any trouble after that.

The expression "of course" indicates that the mother never doubted the effectiveness of her procedure. This is important: the success or failure of any procedure depends often on the expectation of the parent. It is amazing to what extent one can convey to the child one's own anticipation, which stimulates the child to act accordingly.

Margaret, age 7, had temper tantrums whenever she was not allowed to do something, and she became determined to do it. Whenever she stormed and fussed, the parents talked it over with her. Such talk seldom helped. She was then given a choice, "Stop fussing or go to your room and stay there until you come out a different girl." Margaret went to her room many times and came out later all smiles. Her outbursts occurred less frequently.

There is only one aspect of the above situation which resembles the application of logical consequences. Margaret was sent to her room "until" she came back quietly, instead of being sent "because" of what she had done, which is downright punishment. But aside from giving Margaret a choice to return, the situation is typically mismanaged. First of all, parents should not talk with a child during an outburst; no child is willing to listen. It is therefore no surprise that talking to Margaret seldom helped. Second, instead of sending Margaret to her room, which still involves some struggle, it would be much more effective if the mother removed herself and refused to be the audience, without which a tantrum is meaningless. This is the fundamental difference between the punitive approach and logical consequences. We use the expression "taking the wind out of the child's sails."

An 18-month-old daughter, in playing, grabbed a fist of mother's hair. Spanking her did not improve the situation, as she grabbed only harder. After a couple of times of this, mother—in return—pulled her hair, and she stopped. It was a logical consequence; if she could pull mother's hair, mother could pull hers.

Such procedures can be helpful if they are carried out in fun; yet it is necessary not to pull any punches or else the game becomes too amusing. Such logical consequences are not retaliation for what the child has done;

instead, the child learns how it feels and can decide for himself whether or not to continue his activity. When the child hits a parent or someone else, the parent can hit back. People with strong protective attitudes toward children usually object to such procedure. They do not realize that letting the child experience what someone else experiences when he is hit is an acceptable and often effective application of logical consequences.

A dangerous form of involving parents in a conflict is the desire of many boys to light matches. Are there any possible logical consequences short of letting the house burn down?

> Jimmy, age 4, was attracted to matches. On two occasions he was found in his room playing with them. Each time he was warned of the danger. A short time later Jimmy's mother smelled smoke; upon rushing into the bathroom, she found that Jimmy had set the curtain on fire. Luckily, no damage was done, but the question was how to impress on Jimmy the danger of playing with matches so that he would never do it again. After putting the small fire out, mother immediately gave Jimmy another match, and told him to light it and touch it to his hand. When he felt the sting of a small burn, Jimmy was quite frightened and quickly dropped the match. Mother told Jimmy that this would be the result if he played with matches, except that he would not hurt only himself, but also his dog, mother, dad, and any friends that might be in the house. This was the last time that Jimmy played with matches.

Mother utilized the impact of the situation. Jimmy was already impressed with the fire he started. The little experience his mother arranged by asking him to touch the burning match came at the right moment. This probably contributed to the effectiveness of the procedure. One may question whether mother's reference to dog, dad, and friends was talking too much. This is not preaching, but a piece of information of who would possibly be hurt when he played with matches.

Here is another original approach to the same problem.

> David, age 6, was fascinated with matches. The magic of the sparks and flames held curiosity and delight. He never burned things, but he wanted to play with them all the time. He was allowed the responsibility of burning the papers and trash in hope that this would provide a needed outlet and give him adequate satisfaction. The fascination still persisted. Mother couldn't stop and oversee his match-lighting craze whenever it struck him. So one day she asked him if he'd like to come up to the kitchen sink and light matches. "Whoopee! I can have this whole box of matches to light?" Mother said he could; but if he started, he must stay to finish, lighting every one in the box. He agreed. He began with great gusto. The sight, the smell, the unhampered ecstasy of it, was "pure heaven" for the first eight minutes or so. Then gradually the interest and zeal began to lag. He was

"tired," he wanted to stop, and this was "enough." Mother held firm to the agreement—he was to finish lighting the whole box. After remonstrations and protests, it was finally completed. The match fascination was gone for good.

Regardless of how enticing something may be, too much of it stops the desire. If a new salesgirl in a candyshop is allowed to eat as much candy as she can in the beginning, there is no problem of her taking candy afterward.

The following example is unique and highly dramatic.

Peter, age 11, was a firebug. He had set fires several times. On one occasion it endangered the mother's life when she was in the basement. This time he had set a fire in the backyard which spread and threatened the house. Firemen had to come and put out the blaze.

The mother took her five children, including Peter, and had them sit down in the living room in a row. She sat down in front of them, just looking at them, without saying one word. Peter began to squirm. "Mom, say something, do something." She remained immobile, just looking from one to the other. Peter couldn't stand it. "Please, punish me, spank me." She remained completely quiet, despite Peter's increasing agony. Then she dismissed all of them without saying one word. Peter set no fires again.

This is an example of the tremendous power of silence. Instead of telling Peter what he expected to hear and what he had heard many times before, she forced him, by her silence, to think it over by himself. And she not only impressed him but also the other children. She treated them as if they were all guilty. The time she spent sitting with them was time for soul searching for everyone.

Letting all children share in the responsibility for what one child does wrong is an effective method. It may violate our sense of justice, but to treat everyone in accordance with his merit usually has disastrous effects. The parents help the good child to be better and the bad child worse. Only when all children are treated as a group can each one realize that he is his "brother's keeper." (This is in contrast to the present way children treat each other. Brotherly love once was an expression of the greatest devotion. Today one would not wish one's worst enemy to be treated by others as some brothers treat each other.)

Parents find it difficult not only to apply this group form of consequence, but they usually fail to understand why it works. Here are two examples.

Mother had attended a lecture where she heard the recommendation to let all children share in the responsibility for proper conduct. She had three children, 9, 7, and 2 years old. The two older children usually complained about the special privileges granted to the youngest boy. One night, shortly after the mother heard the lecture, the baby was playing with his food and making an awful mess. Mother told all three to leave the table, since they didn't know how to eat properly. The two older children expressed mild resentment, but all three left. From then on, the baby never again played with his food.

Mother was amazed at the dramtic results of her action, but failed to understand why it worked. Why did the baby never play with his food again? One may assume perhaps that the two older children went after him and told him to be more careful with his food. But no; the two older children never had much influence over the baby, and their trying to exert some influence over him now would have only the opposite effect. The baby's response can be understood only if one realizes why he misbehaved in the first place. It obviously was a bid for attention, which he usually would have received had the mother not moved in a different direction. When he saw that his older siblings got the same attention, he was no longer interested in continuing his misbehavior. He was interested only in gaining attention for himself, not for the others.

The effect of shared responsibility becomes even more obvious in the following example.

Charles, age 8, was in the middle between a capable older brother and a "good" younger sister. He was a holy terror. He lied, stole, ruined furniture. His main enjoyment was painting the walls with crayons. Mother could do nothing to stop him. It usually took her hours to force him to clean the walls. When she came for help, she was advised to treat her three children as a unit and to make all of them responsible for what Charles did. This was in sharp contrast to her previous procedure.

Two weeks later mother and Charles returned for another interview. To her own amazement, Charles had dropped all his offensive behavior. He had used crayons on the walls once, and mother asked all the children to clean it up. Charles did not participate in the clean-up job, but neither did he again use crayons on the walls. When he was asked why he had stopped marking up the walls, he replied, "It's not fun anymore. The others are cleaning it up." Charles realized that there wasn't any sense in bad behavior if it didn't provoke a fight with mother. He no longer got what *he* was after.

FIGHTING

Fighting between brothers and sisters is so frequent that many parents are inclined to consider it "normal." (It seems that it has become the norm for children to be "abnormal.") Sibling quarrels are indicative not only of a family atmosphere full of intense rivalries and competition, but of our whole society.

In a fight between children it is difficult to establish who is guilty. Usually a fight is not the result of one child's misbehavior—they all contribute equally to the disturbance. The good or weaker child may egg on the "bad" one, may provoke him in hundreds of ways in order to involve mother. One fights to get attention and the other to defy mother's order not to fight. The children coordinate their efforts, whether for the welfare of the family or the creation of tensions and antagonisms; they present a united front against the parents.

> "For heaven's sake, stop that fighting. You are driving me crazy," mother yelled from another room. "Gail won't let me watch my program," Keith yelled back. "I've got the right to see *my* program," Gail answered stormily. With a sigh, mother went wearily into the living room and settled the fight.

Why are the children bickering over the TV? Mother is annoyed; she says, "You are driving me crazy." This is the purpose of the fight—to keep mother's attention.

The hassle over the TV, which is a serious problem for many parents, could be easily handled if the mother knew what to do. As long as the children fight over their favorite programs, she should turn off the TV until the children agree on what program to see. She must not settle the fight for them; she lets them settle it by themselves. If parents have a good relationship with their children and hold regular family council sessions, then they can all agree on what TV programs to see. A side effect is that parents can help children to reject violence on TV instead of being attracted to it.

> Lucia, age 8, and Calvin, age 5, were watching TV while mother fixed dinner. Calvin shoved closer to Lucia. She moved over. Calvin laid his leg over Lucia's. She pushed him aside. Calvin heaved his full weight against Lucia. "Cut it out," Lucia said quietly, annoyed but still deeply absorbed in the story. Calvin, still watching the show, but not as attentively as usual, began tracing the design of her blouse with his finger. She hit his hand away with her fist. "Cut it out, I said." Calvin giggled. He reached up and ran his finger around Lucia's ear. She grabbed his hand and planted her teeth into his arm. "Ow-w-w," Calvin screamed and started crying. Mother dashed into the room. "What on earth is the matter?" she asked. She quickly took in Calvin's anguished crying and the way he was rocking with his arm held against his body. She rushed over to him, took him up, and pulled him to her. He held out his arm. The tooth marks were very evident.

"Lucia!" "He kept bothering me," she explained. "I don't care what he was doing. You have no right to inflict this sort of thing on your brother."

Mother's support of Calvin, who pretends to be innocent, only encourages him to provoke his sister more rather than to get along with her. Whenever one child screams or cries, the mother will rush to the scene; few mothers can resist the temptation. They are not only concerned with which child is right and wrong, but the harm one can do to the other. It is true that fighting children can hurt each other, but the scream indicates usually a hurt that has already been inflicted. Mother arrives too late; all she can do is provide first aid if needed. But first aid does not have to be administered immediately. It is more important to let the children know that they have to take care of each other.

Mother passed the door of the playroom just in time to see Kerry, age 4, holding a truck over the head of Lindy, 11 months old. He seemed to be getting ready to hit her over the head. Lindy started to scream. Mindful of the wisdom of staying out of fights, mother took her courage in hand and went on past the door. However, she peeked through the crack. What she saw totally amazed her. Kerry was watching the door that she had just passed, and, at the same time, he gently lowered and raised the truck over Lindy's head, barely touching her with it.

The above action is not recommended. When there is danger, one has to remove the danger. If you see a boy about to hit his baby sister with an object, quietly take it away, but without scolding, threatening, or preaching.

The following is a report made in one of our study groups.

Before the parents started ignoring their two children's battles, one child would come running to tattle on the other, and they would jump into the fray and choose the culprit. It was a most nerve-racking ordeal, with mother yelling and spanking. Any one of these sessions made mother feel tense for the rest of day. Then mother started saying to them, "I think you can solve your problem yourself," and kept absolutely quiet no matter what else was said. Very quickly she was able to ignore anything that happened and, just as quickly, the children stopped coming to enlist aid. One day mother heard the younger one say, "I am going to tell Mommy what you did." The older one said, "There is no use in telling her. She'll just say you can settle it yourself." That was the last mother heard. She did not have to take sides anymore, to feel herself boiling with rage when one child took advantage of the other. She learned that most fighting was to get her attention, that parents should stay completely out of their children's fights, not only for the good of the children, but also because it takes away about 90 percent of the tension that child raising entails.

Here is an example of how a mother tried to stay out of the fight but did not quite succeed.

When the youngsters had prolonged disagreements, mother sent them to their rooms and told them they could come out when they decided to be more agreeable. If the fighting started again, they were sent back to their rooms for the same decision.

What is wrong with this procedure? First of all, the mother moves into action only when the children have a "prolonged disagreement," which probably involves some violence. Little does the mother realize what she is actually accomplishing. In order to get mother's attention, the children have to increase the violence and duration of the fight. So the mother stimulates the children instead of encouraging them to stop fighting; she also interferes and tells them what to do. And this game—satisfying the children and defeating the mother—can continue indefinitely.

It is often extremely difficult for parents to ignore intense fighting between children. They "cannot stand it." First, they feel it is wrong for children to fight; second, one of the children might get hurt. But most important is the mother's sense of responsibility; she believes she cannot give the responsibility to the children because it is *her* duty to see that her children behave themselves. Unfortunately, advice to mothers to stay out of children's fights—physically and emotionally—does not tell them how.

We have found the bathroom technique most effective. As soon as a mother feels her tension mounting when her children are fighting, she can remove herself by going to the bathroom. The proper use of the bathroom requires some magazines and a battery operated radio. The mother should close the door, turn on the radio, and take a bubble bath. This recommendation is not facetious, but is presented in all earnestness. As long as the children misbehave, they are deprived of mother's company. And they *do* miss her when she is in the bathroom—present but unattainable. The effect on the whole family atmosphere is dramatic. Children really learn in this way that mother refuses to be the victim of their demand for undue attention and their attempt to overpower her.

Of course one must be firmly convinced of our idea that children fight for their mother's involvement; otherwise it may seem that the children will win out when mother leaves the field. Actually the opposite is true. When mother removes herself, the power and manipulation the children are seeking comes to an end. Sending children to their rooms means mother's involvement and responsibility, but removing herself to the bathroom helps her to avoid both. We have found that other forms of absence, such as going to the bedroom or taking a walk around the block, are not as impressive to the children as the bathroom. This room symbolizes privacy, and children react more positively to this consequence of their misbehavior than to any other step mother could take.

DISTURBANCES WHILE DRIVING

Mother and Eddie, age 5, got into the car to pick up daddy at the train station. It was a bitter cold day, but Eddie rolled the window down. Mother said, "We will go when you roll the window up." Eddie waited; mother sat, impassive. Eddie said, "All right, I'll roll the window up when you start the car." Mother said nothing but continued to wait. Eddie said, "I'll roll the window up when you put the key in." Mother still continued to wait without a word; she was withdrawn. Eddie finally rolled the window up. Mother started the car, smiled at Eddie and asked, "Isn't the sun lovely on the snow? Look how it sparkles, like thousands of diamonds."

This is a good example of how a mother can extricate herself from a power conflict by doing nothing. The automobile provides a great advantage both for children and parents. When the parents pull to the curb and refuse to drive during a commotion, then pressure is put on the children. In the above example the mother did not flaunt her victory, but turned it into a pleasant conversation.

One mother was driving the back-to-school-after-lunch leg of the neighborhood car pool. This involved transporting six to eight children (often all boys) one mile with many stops and turns. She explained her family's rules of car conduct, which included, among other things, feet off the seats, no sudden noises, no fighting. Things went quite smoothly for the first few weeks despite the presence of two brothers who usually fought with each other. Then came the day when they started fighting in the car. She pulled over to the curb and stopped. She didn't say a word. They all got the message. Peer influence came into play, peace was restored, they got to school just before the tardy bell. She hasn't had to stop the car since.

This mother utilized the pressure of the group and the situation very well because she remained completely silent.

For several years Jeff, Bill, and Jan had been labeled the "Traveling Terrors," by their long-suffering parents who alternately refereed and reasoned with their offspring to behave themselves in the car whenever the family traveled to recreation spots. The pattern never varied. Seven minutes of enthusiastic anticipation and enjoying the scenery was the calm period that preceded the squabbling: "Jeff hit me." "I did not. It's Jan. She's kicking." "I'm not either. You guys always get to sit by the window." And from all three, "When are we going to get there?"

Last spring the family established a council. At a set time each week parents and children expressed their opinions in regard to many things, including the "travelitis," which had afflicted them for so long. At one point Bill, age 9, observed, "You and Mom always say, 'If you kids don't quit fighting we are going to turn around and go home.' But you never do." After discussion, all agreed that at the first indication of a dispute among the travelers the car would be driven home.

Three weeks later the family was en route to a zoo thirty miles distant. It was one of the children's favorite spots. True to the pattern, however, after seven minutes had elapsed, squabbling began. Father, who was driving, slowed the car, made two right turns, and drove home, chatting pleasantly with mother all the while. Neither parent seemed aware of the howls of dismay each child volunteered. No one explained; no one moralized.

A few weeks later another "Zoo Day" was planned. Success! No fights, no yelling. As the car pulled into the driveway at the day's end, Jeff made the only reference to the previous, ill-fated outing. There was wonder in his voice as he commented to Bill, "You know what? I didn't even *feel* like hitting anybody."

This example is excellent. Though returning home is not always practical, it should be employed when possible.

FORGETFULNESS

A child will forget things only if someone is around to remind him and to serve him.

One family lived quite a distance from school, so the children had to take their lunch. At the beginning of the year Dolly often forgot to take her lunch with her. Rather than have her go hungry, mother would take it to school, which was quite an inconvenience for her.

Finally one day she told them it was their responsibility to remember their lunch; and if they forgot it again, she was no longer going to bring it to them. This worked quite successfully, for Dolly rarely forgot her lunch after that.

Again one has to read carefully the description. If Dolly still occasionally forgets her lunch, then one can be reasonably sure that mother is still serving her and probably even reminding her; she still feels bad each time the child forgets her lunch. It is not natural to forget lunch, so the fact that Dolly does indicates that her mother is still concerned.

Margaret, age 14, did not choose (or remember) to make her sack lunch.

In the morning she either made the whole group late by preparing her lunch at the last minute, or she asked for lunch money. Finally, mother stated that since there were ample luncheon provisions, she would no longer give Margaret lunch money when her sack lunch was not prepared.

The next day Margaret did not make her lunch and asked mother for money. Mother said she had no change and did not give her any. At three thirty that afternoon Margaret came home and said, "I am hungry." Mother replied, "That's marvelous." Margaret retorted, "But that won't make my lunch. I can borrow the money and then you will have to pay."

The mother in the above situation wonders where she went wrong. She believes that if Margaret borrows money, she must pay it back. Should the mother have mentioned, instead, several ways for Margaret to earn money?

Actually, as long as a tit-for-tat policy is in effect, no solution can be found. First the mother refuses to give Margaret the money; then the daughter threatens to borrow money. If the mother were to point to job possibilities, she would have no tool to "make" Margaret take on a jób, so that in the end she would have to pay for Margaret's debts because she is obliged to do so by law. No, this is certainly not an example of logical consequences, but of mutual retaliation evidenced in part by the sarcastic comment on the daughter's hunger. And the girl gets revenge by retorting with defiance. The tone of voice and the chosen words distinguish clearly logical consequences from punitive retaliation.

The mother must stop fighting before she can influence the child or let the situation exert any beneficial pressure. The mother is not responsible for reminding the girl or giving her money. But the mother needs to plan her course of action. She should not say she has no change, because that is a silly excuse. Once she makes it clear that no one gets any money since everybody can make his own lunch, she simply stays out of the battle. However, this is not so easy since Margaret apparently is in a general state of revolt. She doesn't mind making her siblings late by fixing her lunch at the last minute. There are probably other areas too where mother has to remove herself from this battle, with a friendly but firm determination not to be drawn into a continuation of warfare with her daughter.

ALLOWANCES

Giving a child an allowance should not be a reward for duties performed. The purpose of an allowance is to teach the child how to handle his money. There are other ways a reluctant child can be stimulated to take on chores, as we have discussed before.

The next report indicates that most grandmothers are inclined to spoil children, to give them anything they want. This grandmother was not different, but she was willing to learn.

> Mike, age 12, Jack 10, and Teddy 8, spent the summer with grandma. Each summer the boys practically forced her into bankruptcy. One summer she tried to handle the situation differently. The boys received a weekly allowance. When the allowance was spent, they got no money until the next payday. Naturally, Teddy and Jack considered this a joke. The first Saturday evening they spent nearly all their money on gum and soda pop at the stock-car races. On Sunday when they went to the zoo, Jack and Teddy immediately needed more money to buy food to feed the animals. They were a little surprised when grandma told them, "No more money until next Saturday." During the remainder of the summer the boys were very careful not to spend all their allowance quickly. Much to the parents' surprise, all three boys went home at the end of the summer with extra money they had saved.

It was good that the grandmother learned to say No. The children did not believe her at first, because of their past experience, but they believed her when no more money was forthcoming. (It is characteristic that only the two younger ones tried to get more money; they were probably more spoiled than the oldest.)

> Mother and Nancy, age 14, worked out an allowance program. Nancy's needs were taken into account; she was given enough allowance to cover her lunches, bus fare, school supplies, occasional movies, and afterschool treats. One day Nancy came home with her closest friend, and mother noticed that both girls wore new identification bracelets. She asked Nancy where she got hers. "I saved up for it out of my allowance." Mother said nothing more until Nancy's friend left. Then she berated her, pointing out that she worked hard to support them, denied herself many things so that Nancy could have an ample allowance. She was deeply hurt that Nancy had spent her money on something that was not stipulated in the original agreement.

When the child gets an allowance by mutual agreement, the consequences of such an agreement are that the child has to learn the management of money. He cannot learn this if mother interferes and tries to tell the child how to spend his money. If the child spends it unwisely, he will not have the money when he needs it and that is how he learns, not from mother's scolding.

HOUSEHOLD PETS

Letting children care for pets is a wonderful way to have them learn how to take on responsibility and discharge it. Here is a typical situation in which the mother knows what to do, but does not execute her knowledge.

> Michael, age 11, and Robbie, 9, had begged for a dog for a long time. Finally mother and daddy decided to get one, but only on the condition that the boys assumed the responsibility for feeding and grooming the pet. They promised emphatically. A dog was selected, and the boys were totally delighted. At first they conscientiously cared for the dog, but as the newness wore off, they gradually neglected it. Mother found herself feeding the dog more and more frequently. She prodded, reminded, and preached, but the boys still forgot. Finally one day she threatened to get rid of the dog if the boys didn't do their part. Michael and Robbie responded to the threat for two days. A week later mother resigned herself to the situation. After all, she just couldn't deny the boys the joy they had in playing with the dog.

This always happens: mother cannot apply logical consequences because it breaks her heart to see her children suffer. Actually the mother is teaching the children that irresponsibility pays off, because she is assuming all *responsibility* while the children have all the *fun*. She should not allow the reluctance of the boys to take on responsibility to continue for one day before discussing the situation with them. Mother is under no obligation to interfere with the boys' duties. Thus there are only two possibilities: the dog will starve, or it will be given away immediately. If the boys love the dog, and they do, they will be stimulated to take the right course of action.

GETTING HOME ON TIME

One of the major conflicts, especially with older children, is the time they should come home, either after school or in the evening. Unless there is mutual respect and agreement can be reached, the disregard for time can be a source of constant irritation.

> School was eleven blocks from home, and it was understood by Eric and Jesse, ages 12 and 14, that they would come home directly or telephone if they stopped to visit friends on the way. Parents and children agreed to let someone know where they were going and approximately when they could be expected home. However, the boys could not resist the fine weather, and mother would wait, wonder, and be concerned for their safety. To solve the problem, mother, without warning on a lovely spring day, made sure the bat, ball, and gloves were locked in the house, and took off in the car to visit a friend just before it was time for the boys to come home from school. She did tell a neighbor where she would be in case of emergency. The report she received from the neighbors was that the boys had tried to find an unlocked window to get the ball and bat. However, they did not mention anything except, "We were worried about you, Mom." Mother

didn't have to say anything because they added, "Now we know how you worried about us."

It is generally a good policy to let children experience the same predicament in which they put their parents, as long as it is conducted in the proper spirit, without talking, scolding, and explaining ("Now you know how it feels!"). Such an attitude immediately excludes the beneficial effect of logical consequences. If the children can come home whenever they feel like, so can the mother. Of course it would be wiser to discuss the procedure with them beforehand, instead of springing it on them.

> Sally, age 15, and her parents had arranged that the girl take on the responsibility of deciding when to come home at night. The front door of the house was left unlocked until Sally came in, at which time she would lock the door. However, Sally's night hours became progressively later, until the parents decided it was time to agree on a definite curfew hour. It worked for a few days, until Sally came in later, disregarding their agreement. The parents told her that the door would be locked at the time agreed upon for her to be home. For a while this helped too, until one night Sally came home late and was locked out. This proved to be a very embarrassing situation to Sally and her date; she was forced to knock on the windows, and disturb the neighbors with her yelling, in order to have someone unlock the door. From then on, Sally came in on time.

The parents finally managed to impress Sally with the consequences of her behavior. But the quick agreement and immediate disregard of any rule and order indicate the need to change the relationship between Sally and her parents. Tension in the family atmosphere is evident: "All right, this time you won a point; but next time I will show you that you have no power over me." This is typical adolescent behavior at a time when our youngsters are at war with the whole adult population; the fight rages in every home and classroom. For this reason the above application of logical consequences is not as good as it sounds. The consequences helped to subdue Sally, but did not make her willing to respect order. It is usually difficult for a single family to regulate a youngster's behavior without establishing agreement with his group of friends. The group is united in its attitude toward rules and behavior, while each set of parents wages its futile war alone. To make logical consequences work, Sally's parents must deal with all of Sally's friends and their parents in order to reach agreement.

> Sue, a teen-age girl, had great difficulty in getting in on time after dates with her boyfriend. After speaking to her on several occasions about her tardiness, with little effect, the mother tried a different method. Next time Sue's date called for her, the mother asked him in a friendly way whether he would be willing to help Sue to be home at the midnight deadline. Sue

was present when her mother made these comments. After this, she assumed the responsibility for getting in on time.

This could be considered an example of logical consequences since, if a person can't assume responsibility for himself, someone else should help him. Sue's mother recognized the danger: she avoided sarcasm, the possibility of embarrassment, and the provocation of anger and resentment. A great deal depends not on *what* one does but *how* it is done.

While the problem of coming home from a date usually involves girls, the use of the car is a main stumbling block for the tranquillity of a family with boys. The same principles apply, however. The youngster exerts his pressure and ingenuity to defeat parental restrictions. Nothing can be gained in fighting, nor can peace be restored by yielding. If the family cannot reach agreement, no solution is possible. If there is agreement, it should provide for measures if the agreement is broken. Then a firm and quiet No will work when the agreement is broken.

BEDTIME

Bedtime is not as great a problem for adolescents as it is for younger children. Unfortunately, we have made the right to go to bed late a status symbol. The older a child gets, the longer he is permitted to stay up; therefore many people keep the desire to stay up as late as possible for the rest of their lives.

Here are two examples of the futile struggle revolving around bedtime.

Gregg, age 8, did not want to go to bed at night or get up in the morning. The younger of two boys, he was engaged in a power struggle, with mother usually being the loser. Mother decided, after learning about logical consequences, to ask Gregg if he would like to stay up as late as she did; he could not go to bed before her. He happily agreed. The results were that he not only could stay up as late as mother did (she stayed up quite late on purpose), but he could have stayed up later. The mother asked a counselor, "Why did this backfire? Could this be because we are engaged in a power struggle and the logical consequence has no effect on him? What would be effective?"

The mother is right; her son defeats her. One can see the constant pressure and counterpressure. When mother let him stay up, she also demanded that he couldn't go to bed before her, and he defeated her by saying, "So what?" Her struggle was mild in comparison with the intensive warfare which often rages around bedtime. The first prerequisite is to extricate oneself from this struggle, which is sometimes carried to extremes.

Every evening at seven thirty the battle of bedtime started. Harry, age 4, was a master in prolonging it. "Come, Harry, it's time for bed," mother said quietly. "Not yet, Mother, I am not sleepy." "But it's your bedtime," mother persuaded. "After a while, when I finish coloring this picture," the boy argued. "You come right now," mother said harshly. "You can finish your coloring tomorrow." As mother tried to put things away, Harry screamed and clutched the crayons. Mother, hesitating to fight bodily, yielded. "All right then, finish the picture." Harry again concentrated on the book, a sly smile on the corner of his mouth. Mother sat down on the bed to wait. The child's crayon moved more and more slowly, and mother became impatient. "You are just fooling around. Come on, finish it." "I want it to be real pretty. I have to be careful," was the boy's smug reply. Mother waited a while longer, then said that she would put away the crayons that were no longer needed. Harry protested. Mother insisted. Harry reluctantly let mother put some of the crayons away, teasing her all the while by holding back or pretending to lose some. Once things were put away, Harry found many more ways to delay bedtime. He dawdled in his bath, romped on the bed, wanted a drink of water. Finally mother got him tucked in and returned to the living room. A few minutes later Harry was up again, to go to the bathroom, then wanted another good-night kiss. At nine o'clock he was still active. Mother lost her temper and whacked him. Harry screamed. Daddy came to the door and scolded mother. "I don't see why you have to have all this ruckus every night. Harry, shut up! Get in that bed and stay there." Finally there was peace.

Scenes like this are repeated in thousands of households. Here the child has all the trump cards, and if the situation is allowed to continue, the mother will have no power to get cooperation when the child is older. However, with a small child the mother can act quietly and firmly. The time to go to bed should be discussed with the child, so that he knows when he should be in bed. Then the mother can give him a choice every night to go by himself or to be put to bed by her. If he doesn't undress himself, it is proper under these conditions to undress him, bathe him, and put him to bed. It is a good idea to read him a story if he is in bed on time; children like that very much. But what to do if the child gets out of bed? Mother should pick him up without any words and put him back, regardless of how often he may get up. If she is not upset but firm, he will, before long, see the futility of his effort and stop resisting.

Here is a case of a mother who came close to managing the situation.

Rob, age 3, did everything he could to prolong going to bed at night. Mother had a hard time getting him to take a bath, and an even harder time getting him into bed. He wanted stories read, drinks, or whatever he could think of.

After learning about the new approach, mother withdrew from the situation in the following way. During afternoon play she told Rob bedtime that night would be at eight o'clock and before that, at seven thirty, she would begin his bath. She told him that daddy and she would tell him good night at eight o'clock, and after that they would no longer be concerned with what he did.

The first night wasn't so bad; at least there was no crying. Finally Rob got himself into bed by nine thirty, without pajamas, as he couldn't dress himself. It was on the second night that the problem arose. Again Rob stalled at eight o'clock and mother drained the tub, since he didn't get ready for his bath, and kissed him good night. Rob was still fully dressed and was playing. Then dad and mother began ignoring him as though he were already in bed. He fooled around and began to get into mischief. He took his crayons out and colored on his bedroom wall to get their attention. When this didn't work, he said he couldn't reach the light switch to turn it off. He began to cry but the parents still ignored him by going to the kitchen and playing cards. It got quiet around nine o'clock and mother made up an excuse to go to her room, which took her past his bedroom, to see if he was in bed. He was not in his room, but had gone into the parents' room and was in their bed asleep.

Mother was not quite sure what to do. When Rob had colored the wall, she told him they would discuss it in the morning. The next morning she gave him the necessary things to scrub the marks off the wall and told him she didn't want to see one trace of crayon on the wall when he was finished. When she found him in their bed again that night, she told him he could not sleep there since mom and dad had to sleep there. She told him to get in his own bed. He cried and said he couldn't turn off the lights in his room. She told him this was his problem and was sure he could figure out a way. Rob did.

This mother began correctly. But when she was provoked, she began to talk too much and to lay down the law. Saying she didn't want to see one trace of crayon on the wall when he was finished gave Rob the satisfaction of reaching her and getting even for her attempt to ignore him. The good effects of an otherwise well-laid plan are spoiled. The mother should simply have picked Rob up from her bed and put him back in his without any comment. If she had done that for a few nights, the bedtime problem probably would have disappeared.

BEDWETTING

After dinner mother watched Jack, age 6, closely to be sure that he drank very little water. Every night around midnight, before going to bed, either mother or father awakened the boy and took him to the bathroom. Even then, Jack's bed was frequently wet by morning when mother awakened him. She pleaded with him to try harder to keep his bed dry. Sometimes she spoke angrily because she was tired of all the extra washing. She and the father had tried every kind of punishment and persuasion they could think of. Nothing seemed to help.

Children wet the bed for a great variety of reasons. Some do it to get attention and service, some want to remain a baby, some feel entitled to do whatever they want, some want to punish their parents or the person with whom they have to sleep, and almost all children continue wetting the bed once they have lost confidence in their ability to control their function.

The less fuss parents make, the sooner the child will regain his control. Waking him up at night does not prevent bed-wetting, but trains the child to urinate without being fully awake. A logical consequence is to have the child put his dirty linen in a container to soak, and—if he is older—wash it himself. Under these circumstances he will realize it is up to him to manage his functions; however he does this, he will receive neither special pity and concern nor punishment and scorn.

BAD HABITS

So-called bad habits, like nail biting, nose picking, thumb sucking, and hair curling, indicate deeper disturbances. However, the parents must know how to respond to them in the immediate sense. Are there any logical consequences which can be brought into play?

The basic principles are the same. The first step is to get out of the involvement. Do not nag, scold, and remind, which far from correcting the fault, gratify the child's desire for special attention and acknowledge his power. The most frequently used methods of breaking a child's bad habit are futile; usually they reinforce the habit until it is virtually impossible to break. If a child's bad habit is nose picking, many parents will wait until the child puts his finger to his nose and then slap him. In a little while the finger will be at the nose again, and then the parent will shout at him and forbid him to touch his nose. This procedure, when repeated, will assure this child's bad habit for a long time. But these are the methods by which parents hope to stop him, and they are surprised that they don't get any results. Logical consequences could be to refuse to hold the child's hand, if he is a nose picker, or to sit at the table with him. But the logical consequences must be discussed first, and then applied quietly.

STEALING, LYING, SWEARING

Acts of lying and stealing are symptomatic of a deeper underlying rebellion. Consequently, very few adults can resist the temptation to hit back at their children for these acts. A child who lies or steals is usually trying to "put something over" on the adult. If he arranges the situation so that his transgression is discovered, he is doing it for attention or to demonstrate that he cannot be stopped. All arguments, threats, and attempts to find out the truth are ill-advised. The child who lies and steals knows that he should *not* do it, but he *is* doing it because he enjoys the advantages.

> A group of thirteen-year-olds engaged in stealing books from the library. It was a sport and a triumph to smuggle out books. They saw nothing wrong with it, saying that the library had enough money to buy new books. But when asked how they would feel if somebody took their belongings, they retorted angrily that nobody could do that to them. So they knew that stealing was wrong, but they felt entitled to do whatever they wanted, right or wrong.

When parents know their child is stealing, they should watch for objects to appear which obviously have been taken from someone. If the child is willing to say from whom the object was taken, one goes quietly with the child to the person or to the store and has him return it. If the child does not want to reveal where he stole the object, one can figure out the various places from where it could have been taken and go with the child to all of them. If the child is still reluctant or is too old to take around to possible victims, one can take the object and keep it until the owner is found, but without any verbal onslaught. Playing down the transgression is one of the best ways of making it insignificant and therefore less desirable for the child. This is not permissiveness: one does not let the child enjoy his spoils, but neither does one stamp him as a thief.

The same holds true for lying. Regardless of the reasons why the child lies (to avoid punishment, to pretend importance and success, to try to put something over), one should try to make a deal with the child. Instead of trying to find out what the truth is, suggest to the child that everyone in the family lie to each other. Before long the child will find out that lying is not good, especially if he is on the receiving end. Of course some people will object to such a suggestion. They say that lying is always immoral, and adults should not sink to using lies for any purpose. They forget their responsibility to help children stop lying; being moralistic certainly will not bring about the desired results.

Children feel big and smart when they swear, especially when they realize the reaction their words can produce. The surest way to cure a child of swearing is to let the bad language appear insignificant and trivial, and at the same time to acknowledge his "guts." Instead of arguing and scolding, the parent should sit down with the child and find out how many bad words he knows. This kind of response takes away the fun. Or the parent can ask the child to repeat what he said because it wasn't quite understood. He will find such an approach fairly deflating.

EPILOGUE

The application of logical consequences is one of the most potent ways to influence children's attitudes and behavior. Children learn so much more from the pressure of reality and the situation than from any form of verbal teaching. Logical consequences is one of the action-methods in education.

However, simple as the procedure is, its use poses great difficulties for most adults. The present relationship between generations places the burden of responsibility for what the child does entirely upon adults. So it is that parents, who often are falsely accused of improper motivation of many kinds, do not feel free to rely on reality as a means of teaching children a respect for order and duties.

We have tried as concretely and practically as possible to show the subtle differences between logical consequences and punishment. But it will take considerable time, and a fundamental change in the concept of a good parent (especially a good mother) before the insidious warfare—the vacillation between fighting and yielding, permissiveness and pressure—will come to an end. In this sense logical consequences appears to be more than a simple and effective technique. The application achieves exactly what has been missing; a new order and a new relationship based on mutual respect.

There is another advantage in the use of consequences in any conflict situation. It permits an immediate and positive solution. The method enables the parents to bring about dramatic results in conflict situations which may have existed for a long period of time; suddenly the conflict situation is resolved by the parents' definite action.

It has been stated repeatedly, and should always be kept in mind, that logical consequences are not the only way to resolve conflicts, but rather are the first steps toward reaching agreement. There may be situations where one finds it difficult to apply a logical consequence. In all situations, however, the basic lesson can still be applied, that is, no adult has to fight with a child unless he decides to do so. Refraining from talking, nagging, threatening, and punishing is an important step toward letting the child experience some of the consequences of his transgressions. While one may not know exactly what to do in every conflict situation, it can become perfectly clear to the parents what they should *not* do. This in itself brings about a favorable change in the relationship between parents and children.

This, then, is the purpose of this book: to enlighten parents about what to do in the first and crucial moment of a conflict. It is hoped that the detailed descriptions of many possible steps will provide the opportunity for parents to train themselves for effectiveness. When one can take the proper attitude of noninvolvement, of not fighting or yielding, then results will occur that parents would not believe possible. With a newfound sense of creativity, parents can discover new and perhaps never-before-tried means of letting children experience the pressure of reality. A whole reservoir of potential effective responses may be tapped. Finally, if parents no longer need to spend a lot of time and effort correcting a child's misbehavior, then for the first time they will really enjoy their children.

Parents can time and again reinforce their new independence by reading this book repeatedly. However, our experience has shown that retraining oneself in dealing with children requires more than reading a book. The book should be used by study groups, by groups of parents who discuss each chapter and each aspect. In this way each parent can overcome his blind spots which may prevent him from fully recognizing what he is doing and, even more important, what he should do. In such study groups the examples of consequences which each parent discovers can be shared. Parents may not even need professional help with such help from their peers. One inexperienced mother may not find an answer; but several equally inexperienced mothers together may become efficient through mutual help.

INDEX

INDEX